Praise for
Mosaic

"Amy Grant is a remarkable woman whose contributions to the worlds of faith, charity, and entertainment continue to put her in a class of her own. And in many ways, Amy's wonderful new book, *Mosaic,* is a lot like Amy herself: it sparkles with energy, brims with love, and is blessed with the same deep and beautiful spirit that I've witnessed so many times when Amy has performed for the kids of St. Jude Children's Research Hospital. How like her to have written a book that truly celebrates the magic and poetry of life."

—Marlo Thomas, actress and author

"Amy is one of our favorite friends. Her life is as inspiring as her music."

—Barbara and George Bush

"Amy Grant is a bouquet of Tennessee spring flowers. Not the floral-shop type with ribbons and a greeting card, but rather the just-picked ones. Fragrant. Radiant. You spotted them in a meadow and couldn't resist. Now they sit on the table giving fragrance and color. Amy does that as she paints and perfumes our world with her faith, her music, and her words."

—Max Lucado, minister and best-selling author

"Amy Grant is simply one of the most gifted communicators I have ever known. I've been on stage with her in front of thousands of people—and I've been with her in quiet private moments when she's offered hope and healing to someone in need. In either situation, and in everything in between, I've been moved by her subtle strength and her ability to say the right thing at the right time. In the lyric of a song and now in this book, Amy can turn a phrase like no other. I'm so blessed to know her and so glad that she's sharing part of her life in these pages."

—MICHAEL W. SMITH, singer/songwriter

"I know of no one in our field more generous of her time, talent, or resources than Amy. In my experience, one of the major pieces in the mosaic of Amy's life so far has to be caring about others."

—BILL GAITHER, artist, writer, and producer

"Amy Grant draws from a well of experience as a daughter, wife, mother, writer, and entertainer. Like all of us, she has had her own personal storms in life; however, her faith has never wavered. Through it all, she has given of herself and her resources to help others, and remains an inspiration to millions."

—FRANKLIN GRAHAM, president and CEO of the Billy Graham
Evangelistic Association and Samaritan's Purse

Mosaic

AMY GRANT

Pieces of My Life So Far

Broadway Books
Flying Dolphin Press
New York

To my children

Published in the United States by Broadway Books/Flying Dolphin Press, an imprint of The
Doubleday Publishing Group, a division of Random House, Inc., New York.
www.flyingdolphinpress.com

A hardcover edition of this book was originally published in 2007 by Doubleday/Flying
Dolphin Press.

FLYING DOLPHIN PRESS & Design is a registered trademark of Random House, Inc.

All scripture quotations, unless otherwise indicated, are taken from the Holy Bible,
New International Version®. NIV®. Copyright © 1973, 1978, 1984, by International Bible
Society. Used by permission of Zondervan Publishing House. All rights reserved. Scripture
quotations marked (NASB) are taken from the New American Standard Bible®. Copyright ©
The Lockman Foundation 1960, 1962, 1963, 1968, 1971, 1972, 1973, 1975, 1977, 1995.
Used by permission. (www.Lockman.org).

The Rights and Permissions at the end of the book shall constitute an extension of this
copyright page.

Library of Congress Cataloging-in-Publication Data
Grant, Amy.
    Mosaic : pieces of my life so far / Amy Grant.
       p. cm.
    1. Grant, Amy. 2. Gospel musicians—United States—Biography. I. Title.
    ML420.G814A3 2007
    782.42164092—dc22
[B]   2007027610

ISBN 978-0-7679-2967-7

PRINTED IN THE UNITED STATES OF AMERICA

10 9 8 7 6 5 4 3 2 1

First Paperback Edition

CONTENTS

Every Road

*Every road that's traveled
Teaches something new...*

Heirlooms

*Time never changes,
The memories, the faces
Of loved ones...*

Lead Me On

*Lead me on
To a place where the river runs
Into your keeping...*

Takes a Little Time

It takes a little time sometimes
To get your feet back on the ground...

ACKNOWLEDGMENTS

NOTHING ABOUT MY LIFE would look the way it does now had it not been for the years of creative, emotional, and spiritual investment made in me by Michael Blanton, Dan Harrell, Jennifer Cooke, and Chaz Corzine. Each of us walked into the others' lives at just the right time.

I met Dan in 1971, when I was ten, Mike in 1974, Chaz in 1984, and Jen in 1989, when I was twenty-eight. All these years, in whatever configuration, I've had the security of knowing that I was represented by one of the most highly respected, trendsetting management teams in our business.

Thank you, Blanton Harrell Cooke & Corzine, for focusing your amazing strengths and energies on my career. It would take another book to hold the memories that we all share. Let me say that as much as I've enjoyed the career opportunities, what I appreciate the most about each of you goes way beyond the music. As long as you've been watching out for me, I've been watching you.

Jen, your drive and determination and your ability to be energized by work has made the sometimes overwhelming responsibilities of my job doable. Many of us have benefited from your tenacity, never giving up on a task or a person or a dream (Braden). I've always been able to count on having you beside me in the trenches. You are a true music fan, and that has made every off-the-beaten-path performance an adventure. Your quirky sense of humor, your steel-trap memory, and your ability to tell a story make me look forward to the day when you write *your* book.

Chaz, watching you love and care for your parents until the end of their lives, hearing your constant calls home to check on Deaver and the kids, and seeing you celebrate everything about your children has affected the way I embrace my own family. Of course, you always make me laugh, and I credit you with my best one-liners. You've made connections for me to people and events that I never would have had the confidence to pursue on my own, but your networking goes way beyond the surface. You are loyal and unassuming and have the rare quality of naturally extending the benefit of the doubt, making each of us want to be as fine a person as you believe us to be.

Mike, when I was a kid, just the sound of your voice on the phone, calling our house to speak to one of my sisters, made the mood brighter, making me like you before I'd ever seen your face. Your invitation to come to church youth group changed me forever. During my precarious teenage years, you taught me about the love and mercy of God, about the way he sees me. You've never been afraid of flooding a person with words of encouragement and hope—I've been carried on those waves of inspiration through every stage of my life. Every creative leap we have dared to attempt has been fueled by your vision. Thank you for believing in me for so long and so well that I have finally come to believe in myself.

Dan, I'm so glad you married my sister thirty-five years ago. Thank you for the way you've loved her. If I have stayed relatively unaffected by such a public life, it is because of you. You know and understand me in the context of our whole family and have always provided the bridge between my two worlds of work and home—not just for me but for all of us. At times I have been shortsighted and consequently distrustful about the road I am on. Your cavalier pep talks and candid observations about my strengths and weaknesses (there are some things only family can say) have been the iron against which my iron has been sharpened. You are a good and trustworthy man, and I rely on the strength of your steadying arm.

Amanda and Traci, thank you for talking me off the ledge on the big meltdown day.

Deanna, thank you for twenty-two years of organizing and maintaining my whole life so that I could pursue my creative gifts. Phyllis, it's 10 p.m., do you know where my children are? Dee and Sis, we make a great team.

Dudley, thank you for the opportunity to spread my writer's wings a little bit and stretch beyond the confines of a three-minute song. Your editing ability was inspiring. How nice to be guided by a veteran writer.

Bev, I never could have attempted a project like this one without help. Your love of language, your organizational skills, your respect of schedules and deadlines, your focus, your quiet townhome, our decades-long relationship as friends and co-workers gave me the confidence that this project would be completed on time. Thank you for applying your gifts to yet another endeavor in my life. Chartwell Literary Group is lucky to have you. Of course, you know I welcome any opportunity to share your company and drink your lattes. This experience ranks among the memories of our first garden at Riverstone and our trip to Israel.

Vince, I know you're not looking for a long, drawn-out thank you, but I need to say that your words—spoken day in and day out into my life—have changed the way I feel about myself and about love. Thank you for filling our home with music and my heart with laughter.

You see me for who I am and always have. I see you too, and I love you.

INTRODUCTION

I USED TO ROLL MY EYES when I would hear about someone writing a book just because a deal came across the table. I've always believed that real writers are formed from the ground up. They know from the beginning that they want to write, they dream of writing, they keep their noses to the grindstone for years, they suffer rejection after rejection from publishers, and finally one day, miraculously, they get a breakthrough. Real writers emerge from some magical, solitary existence, having lived an otherworldly life.

Despite not feeling like a real writer, I've always wanted to write a book. Not necessarily one for publication, but a collection of the memories that have occupied my thoughts and become my stories over the years—the ones that have inspired many of my songs. When a publisher approached me with the concept for *Mosaic,* I welcomed the opportunity; however, I soon discovered that thinking about writing a book and actually writing a book are two very different experiences. Suddenly I feared I had nothing to say—that none of my stories were interesting at all. Passing bookstore windows would make me sweat, as I pictured my face on one of those book covers and imagined another passerby commenting, "She's not a real writer."

Then one day I came home to find a velveteen box on my desk. The Post-it note stuck to the top read, "Here's Dumbo's feather. Love, Dan." Dan Craner is an old friend, an artisan woodworker. Inside the box was a beautiful, handmade, wooden pen. When I called Dan to say thank you, he said, "Amy, I don't know what you'll write in this book, but I know you'll discover it as you go. And now let me tell you about the wood I used to make your pen.

"It comes from southern Mississippi, from a tree that was cut down to build a cabin in 1800. The tree was over two hundred years old when the cabin was built. I know because I counted the growth rings on some of the cross sections myself. Just think, Amy, when that tree was a sapling in about 1590, Galileo was under house arrest for claiming that the earth wasn't the center of the universe."

Sitting with this pen in my hand many times since that conversation, I've realized that life is short and people wear out a lot faster than things do. What matters about writing is writing about something you find meaningful yourself. So I began.

I started with the easiest memories to tell: a chance meeting, a succinct experience with a clear beginning and end. However, life is lived on a continuum, and the people in our lives grow and change—mature and age—as do we. The people and stories in our lives aren't always so easy to contain. For instance, I found that every time I raised my pen above the paper to write about my father, I hesitated, asking myself, *Which era of my father? The young athlete? The handsome, brown-eyed daddy of four little girls? The respected radiation oncologist? The salt-and-pepper-haired father of the bride? The retired grandfather? Or the white-haired great-grandfather?*

I found that really all I have to share are pieces of my life so far. As the book began to take shape as a mosaic, I was reminded of something a dear friend once told me.

When I was expecting my third child, a daughter, I wanted to name her for the beloved comedienne Minnie Pearl, whose real name was Sarah Cannon. Unlike the backwoods, hooty hayseed "Minnie," the real Sarah Cannon was brilliant and poised. Onstage or off, she was loved by all.

On the day I went to see Sarah, she was bedridden and near the end of her life. I was two months away from my October 25 due date, which happened to be her birthday. She was in the mood for conversation, and while I sat on the edge of her bed, we talked about everything from poetry to dark clouds and silver linings. At one point in our visit, she asked me unexpectedly, "Amy, do you know what the most important color is in an artist's palette?" My mind began scrolling through the Crayola sixty-four-color pack, thinking of all the possibilities for an answer. Finally, she said, "Child, it's black. Black is the most important color for an artist. You see, without black there is no depth. Without black everything appears flat. But mix black with any color and you can paint an object so real you want to reach out and touch it."

In our lives the darkest times, the days that are bleak and black, add depth to every other experience. Like the dark bits of color in a mosaic, they add the contrast and shadows that give beauty to the whole, but they are just a small part of the big picture. As an artist studies a tree with an eye toward capturing its likeness on paper, I have chosen these stories to examine their emotional lines and curves, shadows and light. Seasons of darkness have made the landscape of my life richer, but I am grateful to say that my days are overwhelmingly filled with light. I owe that to my children, my family, friends, work, music, and the love of my amazing husband, Vince.

Compiling this collection of memories has had two profound effects on me. The first and most obvious would be that I have spent a lot of time reminiscing, and that has made me grateful for all the people and experiences in my life (so many more than I could ever mention in this book). What a gift to work and travel, to live and to laugh with the people you love.

The second is that I've realized how many days pass in semi-unawareness—a kind of busy oblivion. Thanks to writing and remembering, I'm reinspired to value both the mundane and magical moments. Some days are crowded with details, and others with sweet hours of peace and beauty, but whatever they hold, I don't want to miss a thing.

In trying to capture a few memories as best I can, I give myself the gift of treasuring what has been so far a very full and meaningful life.

I hope you will do the same with yours.

WHO I AM

Might scare me to death
Or chill my bones
Break my heart
Or warm my soul
But since I'm here and before I go
I want to find out who I am

Late one cold Thanksgiving night
They welcomed me, another 60's child
Into a family that's holding tight
It's part of who I am

I got a mama who prays for me
She fights the devil down on her knees
I can't see all that Mama sees
But it's part of who I am

She gave me truth and she watched me grow
I toed the line and I test the rope
And I've tried a little bit of everything I know
To find out who I am

Who I am
Does it matter anyway
Who I am
And what I've seen along the way
Who I am

Changes a little every day
But with the light of truth
And an open heart
I just want half a chance
As long as I'm here and before I go
To find out who I am

Music is my soul's delight
It comes to me both day and night
It gives me wings to give me flight
It's part of who I am

I hold on to a simple faith
About the choices and the path I take
That through the good and the bad mistakes
I'm gonna find out who I am

Who I am
Does it matter anyway
Who I am
And what I've lost along the way
Who I am
Changes a little every day
But with the light of truth
And an open heart
I just want half a chance
As long as I'm here and before I go
To find out who I am

Did it ever really matter
In the big forever plan
Who I am and what I'm here for
I don't know
Is it wrong to want an answer
To try to understand

Who I am
Does it matter anyway
Who I am
And what I've learned along the way
Who I am
Changes a little every day
But with the light of truth
And an open heart
I just want half a chance
As long as I'm here and before I go
To find out who I am

Every Road

Every road that's traveled
Teaches something new...

EVERY ROAD

There you go making mountains
Out of such a little hill
Here I go mixing mortar
For another wall to build
There's a struggle in this life we lead
It's partly you
It's partly me, but

Every road that's traveled
Teaches something new, and
Every road that's narrow
Pushes us to choose
I'd be lying if I said
I had not tried to leave a time or two
But every road that leads me
Leads me back to you

Here we stand in the middle
Of what we've come to know
It's a dance, it's a balance
Holding on and letting go
But there is nothing that we can't resolve
When love's at stake
When love's involved, 'cause

Every road that's traveled
Teaches something new, and
Every road that's narrow
Pushes us to choose
I'd be lying if I said
I had not tried to leave a time or two
But every road that leads me
Leads me back to you

Salt Water

I CAN'T REMEMBER THE FIRST TIME my parents took me to the ocean. I'm the youngest in my family, and beach vacations were already a tradition in our household by the time I was able to travel—by car, of course. Just hearing the word *vacation* now conjures up memories of those overnight drives—my dad preferring to travel through the night while my sister Carol and I slept in the backseat. I can still hear the sound of my mother's unscrewing of the thermos lid and pouring Dad another cup, the comforting smell of black coffee wafting through the car. The quiet of the lonesome highway.

Summer weeks at the beach have been part of every stage in my life; throughout all the changes of many years, the oceanfront constants—drip castles, body surfing, people watching, long walks, soaking in the heat—remain.

I've collected starfish, sand dollars, more shells and pieces of sea glass than I can count, and even rescued a baby octopus a time or two. An old friend and I have often reminded each other that there's not much a little salt water can't cure, whether from the Gulf or the Atlantic or a bucket of tears.

Before I developed my current shark phobia, I couldn't just sit and watch the water. I had to be in the salt, in the sand, with green slime and crushed coquina shells stuck in the lining of my bathing suit. Those waves have rolled me up in a ball and sent me crawling on my hands and knees out of the surf and onto the sand, hoping my bathing suit was still intact. I have watched the sun rise and set on the ocean, many oceans, across many seasons. I've watched the water by starlight, marveling at the fluorescent green breakers at midnight. Watched it in the heat of the day. Listened to its crashing roar that I love so much. I am drawn to it and afraid of it. It reminds me of the power of God's creation, and nobody has to explain it to me. Nothing about it is diminished in my absence.

I inherited by marriage three nieces, who by the time they were almost in high school had never seen the ocean. I couldn't believe it. They had seen it in *National Geographic* magazines, seen it on postcards, seen it on television, the intro to *Hawaii Five-O*. But not the real deal. I quickly developed a plan to change all that—a place to stay, a car full of gas, and a map. We made it a girls' trip, my nieces, their moms, and me.

The old Highway 98 into Destin, Florida, runs along the beach for a few miles. Like the way many of the old beach towns are set up, Destin features the ocean on one side of the highway and all the places to stay on the other. After a seven-hour road trip, we drove into town toward the end of the day. The afternoon sun was shining. The sky was a brilliant blue.

I made the girls promise not to peek across the highway. I suggested we drop our bags, put on our clothes for dinner, and go see the ocean. By then it was sunset.

An old wooden walking bridge crossed over the highway between our parking lot and the beach. My heart was pounding. I got to be the lucky one to make this introduction: "Close your eyes. You're not going to believe this."

With eyes closed, my nieces held the handrail, climbed the stairs, and walked across the length of the bridge. We could hear cars passing under us, but above it all, the insistent sound of the surf. When we got to the beach side of the bridge, I said, "Open your eyes."

There was water and sky as far as the eye could see. The last purple glow was fading on the far right edge of the horizon. The wind was whipping our hair, filling our senses with the primitive smell of salt and sea.

The girls started laughing and shouting. The postcards hadn't done it justice. Television and surround sound—they didn't even come close. The next thing I knew, those three girls ran down the other side of the steps, across the sand, and straight into the water with their dinner clothes on. The pull was irresistible.

Salt water is the greatest component of our world, yet some people have never seen an ocean. That doesn't change the ocean. It is constant and powerful, and like the love of God, whether we're immersed in it, standing on the shore, or a thousand miles away, it remains.

LEAVE IT ALL BEHIND

I took a drive along the west bank of the shore
I thought of what you said then I thought some more
You say your life is all but chiseled out in stone
And all you want is just a taste of the unknown

Think it was yesterday I called you on the phone
You say you need a change, I recognize the tone
Buy me a ticket please, to anywhere I'll go
I'm not saying what is right or what is wrong
I'm just thinking you've been hanging here too long

So, why don't we just up and leave it all behind?
Maybe a change would ease your mind
For a time, leave it all behind

What I really want to do is see you smile
Hear you talk and let me listen for a while
There's too much going on to keep it all inside
You try to whisper, but you start to scream and shout
What you need is just a place to let it out

So, why don't we just up and leave it all behind?
Maybe a change would ease your mind
For a time, leave it all behind

You try to whisper, but you start to scream and shout
What you need is just a place to let it out

So, why don't we just up and leave it all behind?
Maybe a change would ease your mind
For a time, leave it all behind

Jack

ONE WINTER DAY WHEN MY ten-year-old daughter, Sarah Cannon, was home from school, I decided to take her with me to look at an old horse that was for sale. My sister Carol and I had a horse when we were younger, and I'm always trying to whet my kids' appetites for things we can do together at the farm.

Sarah was a prime candidate for being a full-fledged horse lover. She just needed a little more confidence around them. I guess riding lessons could have been an option, but neither of us likes to have our time all planned out. I thought if we found a horse that was already dead broke, then we could just trail ride whenever we wanted to. Sarah wasn't as keen on the idea as I was, but she drove with me and our friend Leigh Ann to a farm in Leiper's Fork where Jack was a school pony. Leigh Ann is my oldest friend. When we were kids, we lived across the street from each other, and now we own property side by side out in the country. We've always enjoyed riding together, but Leigh Ann turned into the real horsewoman. She's the one who found Jack.

Sarah never did get on to ride that day. She wasn't feeling well, and I knew I was forcing it a little bit. But I rode. Jack was a Steady Eddie. He was rust colored and shaggy, and I thought he was perfect. We went through the paces in a sand pen, round and round, as Sarah watched from the fence.

Little by little Jack did grow on Sarah. He had an easy canter, and at the farm I'd see her stretch out on his bare back and close her eyes, her face to the sun. She and I never became the big trail-riding duo that I dreamed we would, but we did a little camping and more riding than we would have done without Jack.

When spring came around and all his shaggy hair fell out, we discovered that Jack had a brand on his right shoulder. He had been a workhorse on a ranch out west before he came to Tennessee, and the brand was just two letters, SC. Jack was already Sarah's, but now that we knew he was branded with her initials, it seemed mysterious and wonderful that he belonged to her. Those scarred letters confirmed what was already true.

We have a way of branding each other, of branding ourselves. "He's dependable" or "She's flaky." I brand myself every morning when I wake up and look in the mirror. *You're puffy...not puffy... Getting older... I see gray hairs.* You know the drill. In a culture that worships youth and beauty, the process of aging, even gracefully, is not the feel-good experience everyone is looking for.

I've decided it's time to start reminding myself of some other words that are true. Today as I was brushing my teeth, I saw my reflection in the mirror...no contacts in yet, so I looked softer around the edges. Before my mind started assessing the toll of time, I spoke in an early morning whisper to my forty-six-year-old reflection: "You are made in the image of God. You are the salt of the earth. You are like starlight shining out in the darkness. You're the light of the world."

What is it about these words that is so mysterious and powerful? I am just repeating what has already been said. What is already true.

Love Has a
Hold on Me

I have found the perfect mystery
Love has a hold on me
Long before my life had come to be
Love had a hold on me
Love has a hold on me

Where do I come from
What does life mean
Is it not to know the One who made me

As I'm looking down the road ahead
Love has a hold on me
Someday when I breathe my dying breath
Love has a hold on me
Love has a hold on me

Where will I go
When this life is through
Back into the light that made me and you

I don't have answers to all the questions
Running inside of my mind
But I can't help believe that
Understanding comes in time

Something opened up my eyes to see
Love has a hold on me

17

Dorothy Lee

IT HAD BEEN A LONG, EXHAUSTING DAY. Our new house was filled with boxes and piles of all kinds, but the movers had left, and it was quiet now. Vince was sleeping on the red sofa a few feet away from me, and I was sitting at the kitchen counter. The sun was setting. A calm stillness lay on the place.

For no reason at all I started shuffling through a messy stack of unfiled papers and letters on the kitchen counter. A letter in a scribbled blue marker caught my attention from the top of the pile. It was a request for Vince to send a birthday greeting to a woman turning eighty-nine years old. The note was written by her grown daughter.

I didn't know how old the letter was. I hadn't seen it at the old house, but it must have been there. I wondered if Vince had seen it and set it aside. What was the birth date again? I scanned the page. Today. The woman's mother turned eighty-nine today.

I stuffed the note in my back pocket. Eventually I woke Vince up, and we went to meet some friends. Later that evening, while we were driving around town with some unexpected time on our hands, I remembered the letter. I took it out of my pocket and read it aloud to Vince. It was news to him. He was as intrigued as I was by the timing of it all—that this letter, mailed to our old address, got unearthed in the move and made it to the top of a pile just in time for him to make the call.

Busy signal. So we decided to drive around. He kept calling. Still busy. We kept driving. Busy. Still driving. Still busy. This was crazy. Who doesn't have call waiting in the twenty-first century?

Finally, Vince said, "Hey, where does this woman live? Let's just drive by her house." We found her address.

This was getting interesting. The birthday girl didn't even know about the letter, so the last thing she expected was for Vince to show up at her front door. Just as we were turning onto her street, Vince finally got a ringing line.

He said, "Hey, I understand somebody in this house is having a birthday. This is Vince Gill, and I just called to say hi... No, really, it is me... Yes, it is... That's right. And if you're not too busy, my wife and I thought we'd stop by to say hello." He hung up with a big smile, and we were there, in front of a little white box of a house surrounded by other small houses in a neighborhood crisscrossed with chain-link fences.

Dorothy Lee was a tall woman, though slightly stooped. She was made of old stock, sturdy and angular. A wheelchair was in the middle of the front room, but she was not in it. She was greeting us like old friends at the front door.

When the initial shock of our arrival had passed, Dorothy Lee showed us around her home. The front door opened into the living room, bedroom to the left, dining room and kitchen a straight shot from the front room. Pictures of Vince were everywhere—a magnet on the refrigerator, a cardboard stand-up Vince in the front room, framed clippings on a wall. Dorothy didn't act gooey or silly toward Vince, but one look at her house and you could tell that she was a true fan.

Everybody's got a story, and Dorothy Lee had a wealth of them: Stories about her early childhood lived on a farm in Kentucky, too rural to have a "proper" address. Stories about the children she had raised—hers, her grandchildren, even some great-grandchildren. Stories about the husband she had buried thirty years ago.

Dorothy was born in 1911 and had lived in this house most of her adult life. The neighborhood had seen a lot of change. She grew up in a world that was completely segregated, and she would have been in her midfifties during the legendary civil-rights sit-ins in Nashville.

"I'm the oldest person in this neighborhood," she said. "When I moved here, it was all white. Now I'm the last one on the block."

She told us that people had asked her if she wanted to move. Seeming tickled to talk about it, she said, "You know, I'm just an old woman. I don't care what color a person's skin is." We asked her if she was afraid to live alone.

"What would I be afraid of?" she replied.

Dorothy had a sharp mind and a quick wit. The time flew by.

The conversation turned, and she began to talk about her mother. Her love was still immediate and powerful, even though death had separated them decades before. As Dorothy spoke, I thought about her daughter, the one who had written the letter to Vince. I thought about the children that I had birthed. I thought about the threads of need and love and care that tie us to our mothers, and then I listened.

Dorothy had been closer to her mother than her other siblings had been, not because she was the favorite, but because of unfortunate events that happened in her childhood. For instance, one winter day while she was playing near the hearth, she rolled too close to the coals, and her clothes caught on fire. She was in bed for months, her mother by her side.

A few years later, Dorothy Lee was playing with some children in the loft of their barn, when she lost her footing, fell to the ground, and broke her back. The long road to recovery strengthened the special closeness they shared, and as the years rolled by, the bond between them held steady.

On the day her mother died, Dorothy recalled, her world ground to a halt. She couldn't find the energy to do much of anything. Some days she could hardly eat. Most days she never got out of her nightclothes. She remembered hearing bits and pieces of one-sided conversations as her husband spoke to concerned callers from the phone in the hall: "No, this isn't a good day," he would say, or, "She seems to be feeling a little better today."

Then one day, she said, she got up, put her clothes on, and went about the business of living.

"How long were you in bed?" I asked, remembering an acquaintance of mine who once stayed in bed over two weeks because of depression.

"Oh," she said, "I'd say two or three years, as best I can remember."

Two or three years! I was dumbfounded. Had her husband ever wondered if she had lost her mind? I asked her as much. She said, "He was a good man. You know, you cannot rush grief."

Really? I thought. You can on the surface. We do it every day. Someone dies. Friends and family gather at the graveside. Flowers are sent. Prayers are prayed. Handwritten notes or Hallmark sympathy cards are sent. But these days no one is allowed to check out of life for two years. Instead, we prod and push the bereaved to move on, to go through the motions of living. Grief has its own timetable. What a concept. The time it takes to heal is the time it takes.

My thoughts drifted away to a train station in Africa, back to a time when I was visiting my friend Jeannie, who was teaching school in the western province of Kenya. It was January of 1985, and we were standing on the platform, wishing we had time to grab a warm Coke (the only kind there was in Kenya) before our trip. No schedules were posted that we could see, and we wanted to be on the next train.

Finding an attendant, we asked, "Can you tell us when the train will be leaving the station?"

The tall African man in uniform said, "De train will come up dis track. De peoples will get off de train. You will get on. Den de train will leave."

"I understand the process. What I need to know is the time frame. My friend and I want to leave the station for a few minutes. Can you tell me approximately when the train is expected?"

Once again he explained. "See dis track? De train will come up dis track and stop at dis station. De peoples will get off de train. You will get on. Den de train will leave."

We nodded and smiled. Point taken. When it happens is when it happens.

We continued to talk with Dorothy about her life now, what it was like, who comes by, how she spends her time. She told us that at night when she lays her head on her pillow, she looks back over the details of the day, and every night she asks herself the same question: *Did I live this day in a way that honored the One who gave me this day?*

Then she turned to Vince, who was kneeling on the floor beside her chair. Her face was so full of love and kindness toward him (she had told him earlier in the evening that her friends and family always called her anytime he was on television, knowing she cared about him like a son).

"You know why I pray that prayer, don't you, Vince? It's because one day every knee will bow, and every tongue will confess that Jesus is Lord. You know that, don't you, Vince?"

Stillness. Dorothy Lee, eighty-nine years of life on her face, watched Vince intently.

"Yes ma'am, I know that." My husband wrapped his arms around Dorothy with a strong hug. She said, "That was nice. Could we do that one more time?"

As we prepared to leave, we told her we were expecting a baby. She was, in fact, the first person who heard our news. Speaking of babies made her think of her own daughter. She explained, "Years ago, my sister, who worked at the Department of Human Services, called me on the phone and said, 'You've got to come down here. A family of children was dropped off today. You've just got to come see them.' When I walked in, I saw a little girl about seven months old. Do you know, that child just raised her arms to me, just like that. Well, I looked at my sister and I said, 'I guess this one's mine.' I brought her home and raised her."

That rescued child was the one who had written the letter that brought us here all these years later.

CHILDREN OF THE WORLD

Every life, every beating heart
Has a searching soul inside
Ever needing, ever seeking out
The meaning to life

I refuse to believe that we're only here to live and die
In the futile days of a faithless haze
Never asking why, why would I
When I've felt the hand of eternity
It's a legacy I will leave, I want to leave

For the children of the world
Every single little boy and girl
Heaven plants a special seed
And we must have faith for these

I will stand for the truth I've seen
So that truth is seen in me
I will give from the source of love
So all that I believe is handed down
For the road that's yet to be traveled on
By the ones who will carry on, I'll carry on

For the children of the world
Every single little boy and girl
Heaven plants a special seed
And we must have faith for these
Red and yellow, black and white
They are precious in the Father's eyes
Like the Father may we see
That they have a destiny
And give them the light of love to lead

Through the darkness around us now
To a place where hope is found
For the children of the world

Ask Me

WHEN MY CHILDREN WERE BABIES, I bathed them in the tub with me. Cradling the back of the tiny head in the palm of my hand, I would glide them along the surface of the water as if they were doing the backstroke. Their eyes were wide and watchful. Their arms and legs drifted free, held up by the movement of the water and by the strength of my hand.

When my oldest child, Matt, was born, Bruce Springsteen's *Tunnel of Love* record had just been released. In fact, my reentry moment from the world of blood and water—childbirth and milk glands—back into adult interaction and creativity was the week after Matt's birth, when his father, Gary, brought home *Tunnel of Love*. Matt and I listened to it start to finish.

One song in particular haunted me. It told the story of a woman who waded into the river with her child and put him under the water. I never bathed a baby again without remembering that song. When you're responsible for a child, you have such power over them, and humans are capable of such extremes, of cherishing and destroying.

I'm fairly sure it would take all the fingers on both my hands and more to number the friends I've known who were acted upon in a cruel way by an adult they trusted, either because of alcohol or ignorance or history repeating itself. I've tried to tell some of their stories through songs and poems in hopes that if light were brought into that deep darkness, we could see each other's faces, see the scars for what they are, and find a way out of the cycle.

A few months after I recorded and released the song "Ask Me," I received a letter in the mail from a man who was a father. He had been bathing one of his children the night before while my music was playing in the next room. Unconsciously, he had been slowly moving toward the behavior that had been done to him as a boy. But this particular night, with his own child in the bath and "Ask Me" playing in the background, the man recognized his wounded behavior in the way he touched his son. He wrote to tell me that he wept on the bathroom floor and vowed to get help.

 Ask Me

I see her as a little girl hiding in her room
She takes another bath and she sprays her momma's perfume
To try to wipe away the scent he left behind
But it haunts her mind.

You see she's his little rag, nothing more than just a waif
And he's mopping up his need, she is tired and afraid
Maybe she'll find a way through these awful years to disappear.

Ask me if I think there's a God up in the heavens
Where did he go in the middle of her shame?
Ask me if I think there's a God up in the heavens
I see no mercy and no one down here's naming names
Nobody's naming names.

Now she's looking in the mirror at a lovely woman face
No more frightened little girl, like she's gone without a trace
Still she leaves the light burning in the hall
It's hard to sleep at all.

Till she crawls up in her bed acting quiet as a mouse
Deep inside she's listening for a creaking in the house
But no one's left to harm her, she's finally safe and sound
There's a peace she's found.

Ask her how she knows there's a God up in the heavens
Where did he go in the middle of her shame?
Ask her how she knows there's a God up in the heavens
She said his mercy is bringing her life again
She's coming to life again.

He's in the middle of her pain
In the middle of her shame
Mercy brings life
He's in the middle
Mercy in the middle.

Ask me how I know there's a God up in the heavens
Where did he go in the middle of her shame?
Ask me how I know there's a God up in the heavens
She said his mercy is bringing her life again
She's coming to life again.

Johnny Gillespie

I WAS SITTING ON A BENCH in a narrow Santa Monica park overlooking the ocean, when a man who appeared to be homeless sat down on the bench beside me. It was a very long bench with an armrest in the middle. I had been reading a book and wearing headphones, until I noticed he was trying to get my attention.

"Would you mind watching my bags while I find a restroom?"

I said I wouldn't mind, and he disappeared. The man was middle aged, African American, and could have used a bath. I moved a little closer to the bags and tried to imagine what was in them. A change of clothes? Food? Recyclables? Curiosity has always been one of my strong suits, but I kept it in check until he came back. Upon returning, he immediately started rummaging through one of his sacks until he pulled out a plain glass jar full of juice.

"Would you like something to drink?" he asked me.

I said no. Then he pulled out some food. Was I hungry? No, I wasn't, thank you.

I asked him, "Do you live around here?"

"Sometimes. You?"

"No, I'm a long way from home. I'm in town to work."

"Well, I'm looking for work myself."

A long silence. The bridge stood before us. The question: to cross or not to cross? I made the first move.

"What's your name?"

"Johnny Gillespie. And yours?"

"Amy."

What is it about knowing someone's name that makes that person more human? When we know a person's name, they are no longer just the Homeless Man, the Problem Child, the Cashier. Now I knew Johnny's name. I knew he had a past. I knew he belonged somewhere, or used to.

"Amy, if I ask you for money, say no. I've got a drug habit, but I'm trying to work the program, and money only goes one place."

"Okay, that works. I don't have much money on me anyway."

Maybe because we were in the company of so many other people enjoying the park. Maybe because the sun was shining and the view of the ocean below us was breathtaking. Maybe because neither of us had anyplace else to be, we started talking. Really, really talking. We talked about our families, the ones we were born into and the ones we had started. We talked about the job market, about the music we loved. I asked him if he knew a good place to hear jazz in this part of town. We talked about good and not-so-good people we had known. Johnny had cut almost every tie with his blood relatives. I could not imagine the loss of that connection, but then my experience was not his.

For no reason at all, I glanced at my watch and was surprised to see that two hours had flown by. Johnny must have seen me check the time. Maybe he thought I was about to leave, and so he asked, "Amy, could you spare any cash at all?"

I looked at him and laughed. "You're the one who made the 'no money' comment when we first sat down."

Silence. "Well, I could use some food."

"And you could be lying."

More silence. I knew I was headed for a hotel with a room-service menu. He had whatever was wrapped in his bags. For better or worse, I pulled the thirty-five dollars I was carrying out of my pocket.

"I'll give you twenty dollars, Johnny. I'll keep fifteen."

He took the bill and said thank you.

"Here's how you can know I'm not going to use this for a hit," he said.

"How's that?"

"I'm still sitting here."

We sat and talked some more and had just started our good-byes when three boys (maybe ten years old) approached us with cardboard boxes full of odds and ends for sale. The boys looked harmless enough, but the cookies in their crumpled bags and the slightly crushed candy bars were not for me. But there were other things like tea bags and soaps to buy as well. Johnny craned his neck around in all directions.

"I'm looking for their pimp," he said.

That thought had never even occurred to me. Just as I was saying no thank you to the kids, Johnny spoke up and said, "Amy, pick out something for yourself, something you like."

Johnny's suggestion caught me by surprise. The selection was challenging. The last carton contained candles with star-shaped glass holders.

"How much?" I asked.

"Five dollars each," the boy said.

"Then I guess I can afford three." As I reached for my last remaining cash, Johnny laid his twenty-dollar bill in the box. The boys gave him his change and quickly moved on. We sat quietly for a minute.

"Thank you," I said.

"My pleasure."

"I have to get back to my hotel now."

He said, "Do you want me to come with you?"

I said, "No. Johnny, if you follow me…"

After a long pause, Johnny said, "I'll just walk with you till the path splits. Then you go your way, and I'll go mine."

And that's what he did.

I returned to my hotel room and called my sister Carol, who gave me a familiar reprimand about safety and traveling alone. Somewhere during our conversation about Johnny, she mentioned a phrase from a book she had been reading: "the shelter of each other." For a couple of hours, Johnny and I had shared a park bench, a sunny afternoon, and for both of us, welcome conversation. That was not what I expected. Maybe we both learned a little something that day.

TURN THIS WORLD AROUND

We are all the same it seems,
Behind the eyes.
Broken promises and dreams
In good disguise.
All we're really looking for
Is somewhere safe and warm.
The shelter of each other in the storm.

Maybe one day
We can turn and face our fears.
Maybe one day
We can reach out through the tears.
After all it's really not that far
To where hope can be found.
Maybe one day
We can turn this world around.

Who can trace the path of time?
Not you and me.
The twisting road we call our lives,
We cannot see.
The hunger and the longing
Every one of us knows inside
Could be the bridge between us if we try.

Maybe one day
We can turn and face our fears.
Maybe one day
There'll be laughter in our tears.
After all it's really not that far
To where hope can be found.
Maybe one day
We can turn this world around.
Maybe one day we can
Turn this old world around.

Caribou Ranch

October 1981, *Age to Age*
April 1983, *Straight Ahead*
July 1983, *A Christmas Album*
July 1984, *Unguarded*

PICTURE A RUSTIC COLORADO SETTING: cabins nestled among the trees, split-rail fences lining open fields, aspen trees covering the hillsides. Hiking and horseback riding, hot coffee and fresh cookies, started our days. This is where we made music, in an old three-story log building that housed a recording studio. Caribou Ranch, nestled in the middle of Roosevelt National Forest, was owned by Jim and Lucy Guercio. I made four trips there in the early eighties, taking musicians and their families the first week for recording the basic music tracks, and bringing all of my family and extended family the second week to enjoy the beauty while I recorded vocals.

When I recorded *Age to Age*, the aspens were just turning gold. As soon as we unpacked our bags, we took a long hike led by Mike Blanton, whose idea it was to go to Caribou in the first place. I don't think I've ever sufficiently communicated to Mike how life shaping and creatively inspiring those recording experiences were. No one was looking for success. None of us expected it. We were just loving making music and exploring lyrics and being with one another.

The musicians on that first trip—Paul Leim, Shane Keister, Mike Brignardello, Michael W. Smith, John Goin, Jack Puig, Brown Bannister—were good friends already, but something about those days spent with each other's families allowed us to see each other in a different way. I have felt a lifelong bond with all the musicians I worked with at Caribou. Maybe it's because we never had to get into a car to go home. Maybe it's because we experienced a consistent flow of creativity. All I know is, I've never known anything like it, before or since.

The four trips I made to the ranch were during the most prolific recording years of my life. The combination of nature, family, music, and friends was a pattern that I would have continued for a long time, but just as we were scheduled to fly out of Nashville for our fifth trip to the ranch, we got a call that the studio was going up in flames. I thought about the beautiful old Bosendorfer piano, the worn leather furniture, Paul asleep on the sofa, curled up with one of his red-headed sons, our impromptu listening parties in the control room, dancing in front of the big speakers. So many memories in that place, and now it was gone.

One cold night in April 1983, I enjoyed a leisurely dinner by lantern light with everyone else and then headed off by myself to work on the next day's song. I had a few lyric ideas for the verses of Michael's beautiful melody inspired by Psalm 119. I planned to jot them down as soon as I got to my cabin, the same one I always stayed in at Caribou. It was set back in the trees a little ways up a hill, removed from the hubbub of activity around the main lodge and the dining hall.

On this moonless night with fresh snowfall, I was having a difficult time finding my way up the trail. I am completely night blind. (Actually, I don't see so great in the day either. For years my nickname on the road was a "Helen Keller.") In the pitch black, I ran into tree limbs. I tripped and fell. No amount of squinting brought anything familiar into view. I kept walking, waving my arms in slow circles in front of me to protect my face. Was I even going in the right direction? I knew I couldn't be very far away, but I was panicked anyway.

When I finally stumbled upon the cabin, a fire was already burning in the fireplace. To be lost, even for a little while, made me welcome the light.

THY WORD

Thy word is a lamp unto my feet
And a light unto my path.
Thy word is a lamp unto my feet
And a light unto my path.

When I feel afraid
And think I've lost my way,
Still, you're there right beside me.
Nothing will I fear
As long as you are near;
Please be near me to the end.

Thy word is a lamp unto my feet
And a light unto my path.
Thy word is a lamp unto my feet
And a light unto my path.

I will not forget
Your love for me and yet,
My heart forever is wandering.
Jesus be my guide,
And hold me to your side,
And I will love you till the end.

Thy word is a lamp unto my feet
And a light unto my path.
Thy word is a lamp unto my feet
And a light unto my path.
You're the light unto my path.

Hats

SHORTLY AFTER MILLIE WAS BORN, I scheduled a writing session with Chris Eaton. He was in the habit of coming to the States from England several times a year for songwriting. Even though I was glad to be working with Chris, I was sleep deprived and distracted. Fortunately, he brings a great energy to songwriting, and this time was no exception.

We had opted to work at my house so I could be near Millie, but it was hard to concentrate. Every few minutes the phone would ring. Two-year-old Matt kept running through the room, wanting my attention. Every time we'd feel momentum in a direction, my assistant, Deanna, would call me, or Phyllis, our nanny, would announce that Millie needed to be fed. On my millionth return to the living room, Chris announced, "I know what this song should be about—the craziness of your life."

What a perfect idea. Every interruption became the next line of lyric. Not wanting to lose the momentum of the writing experience deliberating over chords, we stayed away from the piano and the guitar. We simply sat cross legged on the floor facing each other, clapping and slapping our thighs in rhythm, half singing and half chanting the words as they came to us.

HATS

The sun comes up
The breakfast show
Can't you see me running
It's crazy don't you know?
The moon is high
I'm working through the night
Will somebody tell me
Where do all the hours go?

Well it don't stop, no, it's never gonna stop
Why do I have to wear so many things on my head?

HATS!
One day I'm a mother
One day I'm a lover
What am I supposed to do?
HATS!
Working for a livin'
All because I'm driven
To be the very best for you.

The water is hot
The phone don't stop
So how do I manage
To hold on to my sanity?
The red dress on
Time for having fun
But can I really be
The girl you think you see in me?

The spirit is willing but the flesh is weak
Why do I have to wear so many things on my head?

HATS!
One day I'm a mother
One day I'm a lover
What am I supposed to do?
HATS!
Working for a livin'
All because I'm driven
To be the very best for you.

This may be a dream come true
This may be poetry in motion
This may be a dream come true
But when it all comes down it's an awful lot to do.

HATS!
One day I'm a mother
One day I'm a lover
What am I supposed to do?
HATS!
Working for a livin'
All because I'm driven
To be the very best for you.

How did I wind up here?

I ACCIDENTALLY ENDED UP in the music business. Through a series of unexpected circumstances, the same year I wrote my first song ("Mountain Man," 1976), I was offered a record deal. I was fifteen. Chris Christian, the man who "discovered" me, is rumored to have said, "She's not that great of a singer, but she's sincere." I was also clueless.

I booked myself to sing for churches, youth groups, weddings, anyplace they'd have me, along with my songs about faith.

A few days a month I drove to Goldmine studio after school in my plaid kilt uniform to work with my youth-group leader and producer, Brown Bannister. There was no rush and no deadline. My first record came out in 1978 during spring break of my senior year in high school. I autographed album jackets for my classmates at Harpeth Hall the way one would autograph yearbooks. There was no fanfare or publicity around the quiet release of my first record. I was seventeen, and within a few weeks I got my first concert offer.

Brown got the call about the booking and phoned me, so I drove over to talk to him about it. Up to this point, I had only sung for people I knew—family, friends, schoolmates—and the idea that a total stranger would call and ask me to sing for a group of more strangers was mind boggling. Brown said the request was for three hundred dollars.

Three hundred dollars. My mind went racing. I had been saving money for my freshman year at college. My parents were paying my tuition, but I was saving up for extra spending money. As much as I wanted to go to Denver for the concert, spending three hundred dollars would wipe out my savings. I told Brown why I couldn't go. He started laughing and corrected my thinking. No, I did not have to pay them three hundred dollars for the opportunity to sing. Miracle of miracles, they were willing to pay me. I couldn't believe my ears. As it turned out, my appearance at Lakeside Amusement Park, sandwiched between the deafening roller coaster and the fish-feeding area, was the beginning of a long, steep learning curve about hard work, expectation, preparation, and professionalism. I've sung thousands of concerts since then, released over twenty recordings, and watched the music business change drastically. I have some awards on the shelf and gold and platinum records in frames on the wall.

It's been hard work and always interesting. I'm amazed that doing my job led me into the company of so many fascinating people and has taken me to so many unexpected places. Doors that I never thought existed, much less considered knocking on, have swung open for me. That high-school kid (or, for that matter, this forty-six-year-old woman) never had any aspirations for fame or success, but because of the people in my life who dreamed for me and stood beside me and enabled me, I have lived an amazing life.

As I sit here rolling back over the years in my mind, one memory leads to another, far too many moments to recount, but here are a few that make me smile.

I was swimming toward a yacht in the Mediterranean Sea, so far away from the shore that I could barely see it. Several yards ahead of me was Barbara Bush, with Secret Servicemen swimming on either side of her. I've got a healthy fear of sharks and things that might be in the water, but I knew that there was nothing dangerous in this part of the water world. And I'd been told that if I couldn't make it, someone would come and get me. The salt water was so buoyant that I could swim or just lie back and float. Barbara turned around and shouted, "You know, the Secret Service is here for *me*, not for you! So take care of yourself."

Vince and I had been invited to go on a trip that the Bush family has taken every year since George H.W. Bush left office. With them, they take their extended family and a circle of friends of their choosing. They like music, and almost every year they invite someone musical to come along. This particular year they invited Vince and me. And they told us, "Please bring your guitars, but you don't have to sing."

The trip was filled with hiking, backgammon, wonderful meals, and great conversations. Most of those people whose company I enjoyed I will probably never see again. We walked remote, narrow roads on little Greek isles, and at one point we took a bus ride that scared me to death, up a winding road. We discovered a little, family-owned museum. The owner had married an Englishwoman. They showed us ancient relics, and when we left, we promised to send music. (I've yet to send the music, but I still have the address.) At a seaside trattoria, under the stars, we danced wild, reckless Greek dances.

That was not the first time I'd been invited to do something with the Bushes because of music. Twelve years earlier, when President George H.W. Bush had lost the election to Bill Clinton, he organized a farewell gathering at Camp David to thank people who had supported him through his time in office. I was invited to come and sing at a Sunday-morning chapel program. Gary and I went, and my mom came along to help with six-week-old Sarah.

It was a quick trip. We arrived at our cabin around dinnertime on a Friday night and were told that if we were hungry, we should walk to a particular cabin a short distance away. I figured it was a cafeteria or something.

It was dark, and I couldn't get a feel for the place. When we knocked on the cabin door, it was opened by George and Barbara. It was just the five of us having dinner. And then we all watched a movie—*Of Mice and Men*—together, curled up on the sofa with their dog, Millie.

I had met them once before, on a tour of the White House, when Matt was a baby. Years later, they came to a Christmas show and sat in the audience. At the same time, Vince was getting to know the Bushes through his music. He sang at the dedication of the Bush Library.

Life takes some interesting turns. Here in a remote cove, stretched out under the stars around a bonfire, Vince and I sat at George and Barbara's feet, and played guitar and serenaded President Bush on his eighty-first birthday. They watched the stars and heard the waves lapping. It was beautiful.

It was a cool summer evening in Colorado with a tiny mist of rain. Vince and I were at a cookout, along with several other friends, at Christine and Kevin Costner's house in Aspen. The burgers were great. The conversation was better.

I had met Kevin at a fund-raiser golf tournament in Las Vegas several years before. Perhaps to be more politically correct, the organizers thought they should involve at least one female golfer, and I was playing golf at the time. I wasn't an actor, and people had paid thousands of dollars to play with movie stars. Whoever drew my name not only didn't get a movie star but didn't get a good golfer either. My manager and friend, Jennifer, was with me on this trip, and we struck up an interesting conversation with Kevin.

Now anybody who knows me knows that my favorite movie of all time is *Dances with Wolves*. I love its narrative perspective, its setting in history, the cinematography, the exquisite use of empathy. I never imagined I would have the chance to meet the film's creator, but I did, and we talked about the world of acting and the magic of film and music. In the way that one thing leads to another, a few years later Kevin and I sang a duet for his movie *The Postman*, and I even gave acting a brief try. Now, a decade later, I was enjoying an outdoor fire and live music at his enchanting Colorado hideaway. Music brought me here.

Just because I included Mario Andretti's name in a song called "Good for Me," I was invited to watch the Indy 500 from his family's private box in the spring of 1992 (my manager, Chaz Corzine, who accompanied me that day, jokingly asked if there was any way I could include Victoria's Secret model Jill Goodacre's name in my next song). That day after the race, I met team owner Paul Newman for the first time. The mood was subdued because it was a dark day in Andretti racing history: Three Andrettis had started, and none of them finished. One was in the hospital. I was afraid someone might think I had jinxed the outcome, and never expected to hear from any of them again. But Paul's friend and stunt double, Stan Barrett, suggested I be invited to sing at the September fund-raiser of Paul's Hole in the Wall Gang Camp. All proceeds from his food products go to fund this facility for sick children, and twice since that day I've made the trip to Connecticut to sing at the camp.

On my second visit, I met Carole King, truly my greatest musical influence. She was jetlagged from a trip overseas, but I was just glad we got to breathe the same air. Later, I sang on a tribute project to her great songwriting, and she sent me an old *Tapestry* LP cover, signed "Good Job." When it arrived, I ran around the house like a crazed kid, called my mother, then my grade-school boyfriend, Johnny, saying, "You are the only one who will understand how monumental this is for me." Like everybody else, I know what it feels like to be a real fan.

I was thrilled to be asked to participate in the 1987 Prince's Trust concert in London, my first opportunity to work with Art Garfunkel, Robin Williams, and James Taylor. When my family and I arrived in London, I was a brand-new mother of a nine-week-old son, Matt, and we were both incredibly jetlagged. In a brief backstage meeting, Princess Diana gave me some encouraging words as another working mom. She agreed it was worth the fatigue to have your children with you.

Later that night in the dressing room, James Taylor called out to me, "Give me that boy," taking a fussy Matt so I could have a break. I couldn't help but think of his beautiful lullaby "Sweet Baby James," which I had listened to a million times. To this day, I love the honesty of his music. I have been to a dozen of his live shows, and not a week goes by that I don't pull out one of his CDs and listen to it.

My grandmother Grant took my sisters and me to see Tony Bennett in Las Vegas when I was twelve. He was her favorite. Twenty-seven years later, Tony was my guest on a CBS Christmas special filmed in Banff. He was charming and delightful, the consummate gentleman. While we were talking about a particular song we would be singing together on the show, he showed me a painting in progress. It was a landscape. Obviously, his real passion was painting. I used to carry art supplies on the road, and after seeing his painting, I started carrying them again.

A few days after I got home, an enormous spray of roses arrived at my door, with a card from Tony.

There are places I have been just because a video director wanted to film me in a particular spot...perched on a clock tower in NYC...standing under a waterfall. For the filming of the "Lead Me On" video, we were given permission to be in a remote area of Zion National Park. I remember enjoying a cappuccino hot from the catering truck, miles from nowhere. A favorite drink in a rare setting.

I was in a bit of a time crunch during an overseas tour, so on a day off, I flew to the coast of Spain to film a video for "I Will Remember You." As I stood on a rocky outcropping, high above the deep blue waves, it seemed to me that if the wind caught my oversized blouse (pregnant again) just right, I might sail off the edge.

While taping an episode of NBC's *Three Wishes*, I helped a young boy named Colton who was losing his eyesight to see New York City in all its glory. We watched the sun rise from the top of the Empire State Building, hours before the crowds showed up.

During another episode of *Three Wishes*, my son, Matt, and I experienced zero gravity over the Atlantic Ocean on a NASA training flight, granting the wish of a young man from Cincinnati who plans to become an astronaut. That was the greatest "take your kid to work" day of my life (and neither one of us threw up).

I've received a letter from each of our last seven presidents, and I've had conversations with Rosa Parks and Coretta Scott King.

I've won a golf tournament with Bill Murray, and shared a dressing room with Carly Simon and Loretta Lynn.

I've met most members of the Grand Ole Opry.

I've played golf with Arnold Palmer.

My favorite collection of photographs is of my daughter Millie and me—a gift from Annie Leibovitz.

When I was in my late teens, I was invited to be a part of a Billy Graham crusade in Nashville, Tennessee. The football stadium was packed, and it was without a doubt the largest crowd I had stood in front of up to that point. I hardly remember meeting Dr. Graham then, I was so overwhelmed by the situation.

I have been a part of several Billy Graham crusades since then. The last one was in Minneapolis in the late nineties. Before the evening started, I had a chance to visit with Billy. I felt pretty sure I was headed for a divorce, though no one knew it but me, and out of respect, I felt like I needed to tell him that my life was derailing. His organization sets a high standard. If I was going to stand on his stage as an invited guest, I didn't want anyone to be taken by surprise by later events. He talked to me about his own children, reminding me that God is always at work in our lives, even when we take the long way home. The good news of the gospel was as powerful in the tiny curtained-off backstage area where we spoke as it was in the full-to-capacity stadium that night.

Unique gifting brings some people's lives to the forefront. That's true in every arena. I've been fortunate to have had wonderful interactions, both onstage and off, with many people whose work has had a profound influence on my life.

I know that these doors were opened to me because of music. The opportunities have left me thrilled and dumbstruck, verbose and tongue-tied, and always feeling like I'm in a little bit over my head.

And curious about what's around the next corner.

Heirlooms

Time never changes,
The memories, the faces
Of loved ones...

HEIRLOOMS

Up in the attic,
Down on my knees.
Lifetimes of boxes,
Timeless to me.
Letters and photographs,
Yellowed with years,
Some bringing laughter,
Some bringing tears.

Time never changes,
The memories, the faces
Of loved ones, who bring to me,
All that I come from,
And all that I live for,
And all that I'm going to be.
My precious family
Is more than an heirloom to me.

Wisemen and shepherds,
Down on their knees,
Bringing their treasures
To lay at his feet.
Who was this wonder,
Baby yet King?
Living and dying
He gave life to me.

Time never changes,
The memory, the moment
His love first pierced through me,
Telling all that I come from,
And all that I live for,
And all that I'm going to be.
My precious Savior
Is more than an heirloom to me.

My precious Jesus
Is more than an heirloom to me.

Mom

Journal Entry
Summer 2004
Flight to L.A.

Two days ago when I stopped by to see Momma during my
bike ride, she looked so beautiful with her clear blue eyes and
open, genuine smile—not the forced one that goes along with
pain (in the body or in the mind) but the dazzling one, the
one I've always loved.

She was twenty-nine when she carried me. That sounds young
to me now. Four girls in eight and a half years. I was the baby.
Larry, her younger brother, the apple of her eye, died two-and-
a-half years before I was born. I often wondered how that
changed my mother.

Mom and Dad went out every Saturday night, usually to par-
ties (which my dad pretended to dread), leaving my cousin
Glenda and us to watch Red Skelton, My Three Sons, and Carol
Burnett. I don't know the other places they went, but I can still

remember the scent of Guerlain's L'Heure Bleue and my mother
entering the room. She might have been dressed in a pantsuit
or a ball gown, but she was an absolute beauty.

Our home was a welcoming place, with friends and music
and meat on the grill, family meals—formal and not so formal. Every morning I watched my mom in a housecoat cook
a hot breakfast, usually sausage and eggs (scrambled), sometimes Cream of Wheat (my favorite), bacon and jelly sand-
wiches on toast, or pancakes on Saturday (leftover ones would
sit on the stove and be picked up to eat on the run all day).

I loved our house on Shy's Hill where we caught lizards in the
raised part of the car turnaround and buried peach pits in
the dirt between the carport and the woods. We loved making
"houses" in the underbrush of the woods with "rooms" and
"hallways." Momma used to fuss at us about her missing
spoons—not the teaspoons, but the tablespoons. They were the
best for digging. They were also good as peanut butter scoopers.
Many afternoons I would dash through the kitchen to pick up
a spoonful of peanut butter on my way out to the neighborhood. No wonder her spoons went missing.

I remember my mother's young hands, especially during
church, when she would roll my fingers one at a time between
her thumb and pointer finger, starting at the base and going
out to the tip. I loved that. Both of our hands had prominent
veins, but hers really popped out underneath her delicate skin.
I would trace the pattern of those blue lines with my finger
over and over while the sermon went on and on. Sometimes I

would listen—sometimes not. There was a lot of comfort to be found in the routine of Sundays, sitting body to body on the church pews, the sunlight pouring in through the windows.

I've been so remiss about calling and dropping by that when I hugged my mother the other day, I burst into tears. With her arms around me, she said, "Not a day goes by that I don't think of you. I love you. And whether you call or don't call doesn't change that love one bit." She didn't even get choked up saying it. As I'm writing this, I recall how teary my mom would get when I was younger. It used to bug me so much that when my own young-woman emotions welled up, I would dig my fingernails into the palm of my hand to keep from crying.

Now look at us—we've switched. I'm the crier.

SAY ONCE MORE

Let me say once more that I love you,
Let me say one time, maybe two,
That I love the way that you love me,
And I wish I knew more of you.

Tell me that time can't erase
This look of love on your face.

Let me say once more that I need you,
One more time or just maybe two.
That my life will always be richer
For the time I've spent here with you.

Let me say once more that I love you,
Let me say one time, maybe two,
That I love the way that you love me,
And I wish I knew more of you.

Tell me that time won't erase
The way that my heart sees your face.

I call your name,
You look my way,
It's clear you trust each word I say.
When life is long and problems come,
You'll always be my only one.
So now we're standing face to face,
And with one look your eyes embrace me.
Squeeze away each haunting fear,
And say the words I long to hear...

Tell me that time won't erase
This look of love.

Let me say once more that I love you,
Let me say one time, maybe two,
That I love the way that you love me,
And I wish I knew more of you.

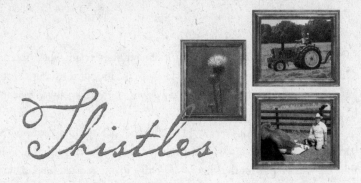

Thistles

Have you ever seen thistles in bloom? They are lovely lavender blossoms on long slender stalks, with silver-tipped prickles on the leaves and stems. They used to be one of my favorite flowers until I lived on a farm and learned that if the blooms go to seed, one plant can eventually take over an entire pasture. The summer my son, Matt, was almost three years old, he and I spent a few long, hot days clearing our fields of thistles with his grandpa Terry Chapman. Terry and Mary had recently moved from Weatherford, Oklahoma, to our farm in Tennessee to help us manage the growing demands of work and family. In addition to the upkeep of the farm, they were thrilled to be so close to Matt and his little sister, Millie.

There are several ways to deal with thistles. One is to cut them down and burn them before they go to seed, but in essence, you've simply pruned the stalk, encouraging a bigger root. You can bush-hog a field, making it good immediately, but the seedpods dry on the ground, the wind comes up, and then you've only dispersed your problem across a broader area. The only true remedy is to put on work gloves and pull them out by the root...or hire someone else for the grueling job. For whatever reason, this particular year, the thistles really bugged me, and I decided to take care of it myself, or at least start the job, with my father-in-law.

Terry had spent the majority of his life as an Assembly of God preacher. Somewhere in the process he mellowed into a gentle storyteller and conversationalist who intentionally or unintentionally taught lessons about life and faith in the context of everyday living. Pulling thistles is hard work. You dig and pull and pry and try to avoid the longest prickles, but the nature of the job makes for good conversation. You can't be in a hurry. It's going to take the hours it's going to take.

As the hours passed, Terry and I watched our pile of thistles grow in the back of the old orange and white farm truck while Matt crawled around in the dirt. We marveled at the singular carrotlike root that could support such a tall stalk. We sweated and laughed and talked for hours on end. And we made progress. Eventually we cleared the front pasture, just east of the house.

Terry's family had worked on farms his entire childhood. Every fall, he and his five brothers, father, and mother would leave Red River County and travel to West Texas to pick cotton until Christmas. He reminisced about the sight of his mother pulling a cotton sack down the row she was picking, his baby sister asleep in her mother's shadow. His stories of hard work and childhood mischief, of Sunday afternoons spent with other boys trying to hang on to the back of a bull calf, of long days and blessed, restful evenings painted pictures in my mind of a time different from the one I had known growing up.

We talked about life lessons that are learned in conjunction with the land, the changing of seasons, and the miracle of seeds sprouting and growing and yielding fruit. We talked about the patterns in nature, patterns of living and dying. At one point when I was struggling with a particularly tall thistle with a stubborn root, Terry called out to me, "You know, Amy, sin is a lot like that thistle you are wrestling with. It can look so beautiful to the eye, be so pleasing to the senses, you hardly notice the seeds are spreading until whole fields are taken over by them. Then they choke out the grass. Animals won't eat 'em. You can't cut 'em down and leave the root. They'll come right back. There is nothing to do but take the time and energy required to pull them out in one piece and fill the hole with something good."

I've thought about those days many times since then. My son has grown. The farm belongs to someone else now. But Terry's words are as fresh and alive in me as they were all those years ago, because they are true. I have had seasons of cleared fields and seasons of thistles in my own life, and thankfully some good, steady wisdom from an old Assembly of God preacher who took the opportunity to teach me about the time and energy required to do the clearing, and that part of life is learning to fill the holes with something good.

Several years after those days spent pulling thistles, I was asked to sing at the wedding of a friend's sister. She was an older bride, had grandchildren of her own. She was also a painter. When I arrived at the church on the day of her wedding, she handed me a wrapped canvas, her gift to me for singing. She said, "Amy, I stood in front of that canvas and asked God to help me think of something that would matter to you, something I could paint. I felt a little doubtful about painting weeds, but I wanted to say thank you." Inside the wrapping was an oil painting of thistles in bloom at sunset.

How Can We
See That Far?

We said our promises by candlelight
You held my hands, I was dressed in white
We were young
How can we see that far?
How can we see that far?

I knew I wanted you like no one else
I told my momma that I'd found myself
In your eyes
How can we see that far?
How can we see that far?

But like your daddy said
The same sun that melts the wax can harden clay
And the same rain that drowns the rat will grow the hay
And the mighty wind that knocks us down
If we lean into it
Will drive our fears away.

And when I woke you in the dead of night
To hold my hands, push away the fright
Life had come—a son
How can we see that far?
How can we see that far?

Yeah, we were nervous and a little scared
Until the music of our baby's cry
Filled the air
How can we see that far?
How can we see that far?

But like your daddy said
The same sun that melts the wax can harden clay
And the same rain that drowns the rat will grow the hay
And the mighty wind that knocks us down
If we lean into it
Will drive our fears away.

We might die
We might live
We could hurt each other badly
Do things, things so hard to forgive
And if time is not our friend
Your mind might forget me before the end
And oh, I cannot
I cannot look that far.

Saved by Love

MY FIRST PREGNANCY ENDED IN MISCARRIAGE at nine weeks, but not before it had been announced on national television (not the way I had intended for my grandmother to hear the news). And so for several weeks I was congratulated by strangers in airports, at the grocery, in malls, and on the street about the good news that was not so good anymore. Consequently, the second time I turned the stick pink, I kept the news to myself for sixteen weeks. During that time my sister Carol found out she was expecting her second child. It killed me not to share my news with her, especially during one phone call when she admitted she felt guilty that she was pregnant instead of me.

As it turned out, we delivered our babies one day apart in hospital rooms next to each other's. After visiting hours on the night she had Claire, we sat cross legged on her bed straddling ice packs, our babies propped up against the pillows like twins.

I wrote most of the lyrics to "Saved by Love" riding around Nashville on a rainy day—my young son, Matt, in his car seat, quieted by the rhythm of the windshield wipers. My inspiration was my sister Carol, even though I renamed her "Laura" in the song.

SAVED BY LOVE

Laura loves her little family,
And she's the kind of woman who loves them with her life.
But sometimes in the evening,
When the world rests on her shoulders
With four walls closing in,
She'll close her eyes.

It's not like she misses being younger,
Though she never was in *Vogue* magazine or on *TV*;
Her husband loves her dearly,
And the morning shows her clearly,
Kisses her little baby girl.
Laura, she's the queen of the world.

Can't imagine ever leaving now,
Now that she's been saved by love,
Saved by love, saved by love.
Listen to her quiet heart singing loud.
Laura, she's been saved by love,
Saved by love, saved by love.
I know that she's been saved by love,
Saved by love, saved by love.
Saved by love.

There's nothing quite like my family's love to warm me,
And nothing short of death's gonna ever leave me cold.
Still, at times, it's lonely,
But through it all it only
Makes me love Jesus more,
This is what he came here for.

I can't imagine ever leaving now.
Now that I've been saved by love,
Saved by love, saved by love.
He's gone and turned my crazy world back around,
And I've been saved by love,
Saved by love, saved by love.
I know that I've been saved by love,
Saved by love, saved by love.

Baby Baby

KIDS ARE WHO THEY ARE the minute they are born. As parents, we have the fascinating job of slowly discovering them.

Phyllis, my dear friend and my children's nanny, was driving in the car with Matt, Millie, and Sarah when they were small. One of them saw some road kill ahead and shouted, "Slow down! Slow down!" Phyllis slowed the car to a crawl so the children could get a good view of the flattened possum as they passed by. As soon as they were clear of the carcass, Matt started shouting, "Whoa, did you see his guts hanging out all over the road? That was awesome!"

To which Millie responded, "How could anyone do such a cruel thing, hit an innocent animal? They could have slowed down. That's so sad."

Little four-year-old Sarah finally piped up and in an optimistic voice said, "At least he still had all his teeth."

Years later, Matt, Millie, Sarah, baby Corrina, and I were wedged in a fast-food line, parked at the speaker box. I was trying to collect all the different orders, burgers, no onions, french fries, extra salt, no pickles. Some fast-food restaurants cater to special orders. This one did not. We were holding up the line.

Finally everyone but Corrina had ordered. I was out of patience as I locked eyes with my silent two-year-old in the rearview mirror. With deliberate calm, I said, "Corrina, what do you want? If you don't say something right now, you're getting a cheeseburger and fries."

All this time she'd been rubbing her thumb and fingertips together. Suddenly she stopped and pointed both index fingers at my reflection in the rearview mirror, and said, "I'll take the money."

BABY BABY

Baby baby
I'm taken with the notion
To love you with the sweetest of devotion.

Baby baby
My tender love will flow from
The bluest sky to the deepest ocean.

Stop for a minute
Baby, I'm so glad you're mine,
You're mine.

Baby baby
The stars are shining for you
And just like me I'm sure that they adore you.

Baby baby
Go walking through the forest
The birds above a' singing you a chorus.

Stop for a minute
Baby, they're so glad you're mine
And ever since the day you put my heart in motion
Baby, I realize that there's just no getting over you.

Baby baby
In any kind of weather
I'm here for you always and forever.

Baby baby
No muscle man could sever
My love for you is true and it will never

Stop for a minute
Baby, I'm so glad you're mine
And ever since the day you put my heart in motion
Baby, I realize that there's just no getting over you.

Coloring

On rainy days my favorite thing
Is a good friend beside me coloring.
She might draw a wolf eating sheep
While I will scribble and scratch and keep
On wadding papers I throw to the floor.
I'd like to draw something my friend will adore.
Would she really like a birdnest with eggs?
Or a wrinkled pig with stubby legs?
Of course, she'll say, "You draw better than me!"
And I will think she's blind and can't see.
I like her picture a lot more than mine.
She got all the good crayons I couldn't find,
Leaving me black ones, and brown and gray,
Colors that look a lot like this day.
But even so my favorite thing
Is a good friend beside me coloring.

The Wishbone

It's common knowledge, I suppose,
That nothing should go up your nose.
But I'm afraid someone forgot
To tell this news to one poor tot.
One day when Pete was all alone
He snorted up a wishing bone.
It was a foolish thing to do
But he was lonely and feeling blue.
Of course it stuck just halfway in
Hanging almost to his chin.
Little Pete was awfully scared
His mother just as unprepared
As, pulling in the drive she saw
The bone that stretched from nose to jaw
Of darling little Peter's face
A memory she could not erase.
And so she said, "Pete, hold your breath,
And make a wish. I'll do my best."
She pulled so hard the bone broke free
And Pete was hopeful as could be.
For he had kept the longer end
And he was wishing for a friend.

Tennessee State Fair

WHEN I WAS IN GRADE SCHOOL, classes were cancelled for an entire day each September so we could have the opportunity to go to the state fair. This day off in early fall was a highlight for all of us kids.

I enjoyed the rides, but mostly I was drawn to the freak shows. Usually I just stood in the midway and looked at the posters, listened to the noises crackling over the loudspeakers, and watched the hawkers inviting people into the tents. Sometimes I was brave enough to go in, but not to see a freak that was a human. Looking at someone and ogling over something that he couldn't help just seemed too rude to me. But I didn't mind staring at animals. I've seen a two-headed cat, a two-headed bull calf, a five-legged cow, a five-legged goat, and a few other weird things in formaldehyde that defy description. Understandably, I did not want my children to miss out on such world-class entertainment.

So one fall day when Matt was seven, Millie was four, and Sarah was just a toddler, I decided it was time for them to experience the state fair. As the kids and I approached the fairgrounds, my mind went back to those days, and I wondered what my children would find interesting now. I was not at all surprised by their attraction to the freak shows. I was still pretty fascinated by all that myself.

On our drive over, I had imagined an afternoon full of thrills and wonder, but the reality was that there aren't many amusement park rides that a seven-year-old, a four-year-old, and a two-year-old in a stroller can do together. The few rides that Matt and Millie agreed upon they enjoyed immensely. With my memories of the fair twenty years earlier, I was shocked at the prices. I had walked in with a hefty wad of twenty-dollar bills in my pocket and was amazed at how quickly that money evaporated. I guess that's just the price of making memories.

The rides didn't last long. I'm prone to motion sickness, so I was happy to have Sarah to watch so I could avoid the Tilt-A-Whirl and the Scrambler. Eventually we were running out of energy, out of cash, out of daylight, and out of diapers. So we decided to buy some cotton candy and head toward the parking lot.

On the way out we passed a climbing wall. It was a simple device—a fabricated wall with rock outcroppings. Two people could climb at a time. It wasn't a race but sort of felt like one. The kids were enamored with the whole picture and begged to climb.

Matt, brave and adventuresome, with his sure love of a crowd, scampered up the wall like a monkey. His was a quick and painless trip to the top, and he rang the bell before the child next to him was even halfway up.

Now it was Millie's turn. I stood beside Sarah's stroller with every protective instinct in me leaning toward Millie. At four and a half, Millie was quite small. Even though Sarah was almost three years younger, at times people asked me how old my twins were. Millie was not old enough to be offended by this comment until years later. She has a petite body, but she has a core of steel.

The ticket taker took more money, strapped Millie into the harness, and guided her toward the wall. Slowly and steadily, my quiet, tentative child reached and stretched, climbed and clung, to the first rock outcropping in the wall. Every extension of her arms seemed just barely adequate to reach the next safe handhold. Each time she lifted her foot off one resting place, it seemed like forever before she found the next firm footing.

The other climber alongside Millie quickly reached the top and hurried down. My daughter remained alone on the wall. I could see her legs shaking,

The Grant Family, 1966

Enjoying time with Great Mimi, my great-grandmother,
Mrs. A. M. Burton

My high-school graduation photo
from Harpeth Hall, 1978

Classmates from Harpeth Hall

Dad, Mom, and my sisters—Carol, Mimi, and Kathy—recording *Rock of Ages*

Mom and Dad today

The "grayshirts" from the Loft

My sisters

With band member Jerry McPherson on the night before Matt's birth

Back in the studio with three-day-old Matt

Matt experiencing zero gravity during a filming of *Three Wishes*

At the beach in 2003 with Jenny, Matt, Millie, Sarah, and Corrina

The kids on Christmas morning, 2004

Welcoming Corrina Grant Gill, 3:00 a.m., March 12, 2001

Swinging Corrina on the beach, 2007

Wyoming summer of 2001

Vince fishing at the Costners' ranch in Aspen, 2006

Backstage with Vince, 2003

Vince and his mom, Jerene

Have guitar…will travel

The cabin—my favorite getaway writing spot

Tour shot from *Unguarded*, 1986

Lead Me On tour with Michael W. Smith and Gary

Matt handing me a flower on stage during the *Lead Me On* summer tour—I was pregnant with Millie at the time

Tour shot from *Lead Me On*, 1988

Receiving the Pax Christi Award from Abbot Timothy Kelly

With Minnie Pearl and the Fairfield Four at "April Evening," a benefit for the American Cancer Society at Riverstone Farm

Backstage with friends and performers during the first of many Tennessee Christmas fund-raisers for the Nashville Symphony

Songwriting trip in 2000 to Florida for *Simple Things*
(Keith Thomas, Beverly Darnall, Vince, Jerry McPherson, and Jeremy Bose)

My career-long managers—Chaz Corzine, Dan Harrell, Jennifer Cooke,
and Mike Blanton—at the Hollywood Walk of Fame dedication in 2006

In Banff with Tony Bennett, CBS Christmas special, 1999

Visiting with Billy Graham in Flushing Meadows, New York, 2005

Meeting the Clintons with Millie at the G8 leaders conference in Denver, Colorado, in 1997

Serenading the Bushes in Greece, 2005

The Indy 500—in 1992 with Gary, Mario Andretti, and Michael Andretti

Playing golf with Michael Jordan and Tom Ridge

Performing at the Columbine High School memorial service

In Guatemala with Compassion International, 1998

her tiny fingers working their way around each crevice to find a safe grip, her big eyes never looking down at the crowd that was slowly gathering. I almost forgot to breathe as she neared the top, my throat tightening.

I hadn't noticed the older woman standing by my shoulder until she leaned into me and asked, "What is that child's name?" Her southern drawl reminded me of pressed linen hand towels and mint tea.

"Her name is Millie."

"Milleh," she repeated under her breath.

Now all eyes were on Millie. She had made it to the top of the wall and was extending her arm up to ring the bell, but the rope attached to the bell was just outside her reach. She reworked her footing and stretched up again. The cord remained just beyond her fingers.

Quite unexpectedly, the woman next to me began shouting out, "Reach foah it, Milleh! Reach foah it!"

Within moments Millie did just that and got hold of the cord and rang the bell. I was speechless on the ground—too choked up to cheer for my child and so moved that this total stranger had stopped to encourage my little one at the top of the wall.

It's funny, when my kids and I reminisce about the Tennessee State Fair, not one of the five-dollar thrill rides is mentioned on the top-ten list of best memories. None of the freaks or oddities come to mind. They've all dimmed in our memories. But we still speak about the white-haired woman with the elegant southern drawl and her words of encouragement. In fact, those words live on even now as I see my almost-grown daughter stretching and pulling toward her own independence, toward the journey of life that awaits her. I stand back, throat a little tight, and find myself saying, "Reach for it, Millie."

MIMI'S HOUSE

I remember many times when I was just a child,
How I played in that old house out on the farm.
With rocking chairs and squeaky stairs, all pieces of her world,
And a fire in her room to keep us warm.

No one is a stranger in Mimi's house,
'Cause love has made his home there in her heart.
And she's got that infectious way of laughing right out loud
That takes away my pain and lights the dark.

And now I'm not as young as when I played there all the time,
And the visits seem too scarce and far between,
But life goes on at Mimi's house, and in my mind I'm there,
With a fire in her room to keep us warm.

No one is a stranger in Mimi's house,
'Cause love has made his home there in her heart.
And she's got that infectious way of laughing right out loud
That takes away my pain and lights the dark.

And when I stop and think of how she's aging,
Growing strong and graceful in her God.
Well, you know it takes my fear away from aging;
She seems to know the secret that we'll never be apart.

'Cause no one is a stranger in Mimi's house,
'Cause love has made his home there in her heart.
And she's got that infectious way of laughing right out loud
That takes away my pain and lights the dark.

Yes, she's got that infectious way of laughing right out loud
That takes away my pain and lights the dark.

Uncle Larry

I LOVE FAMILY. I LOVE BEING IDENTIFIED in the context of my family.

"Oh, you're one of the Grant girls."

"Honey, I knew your great-grandparents."

"Why, you must be Burton and Gloria's daughter."

"Your father was my mother's doctor. He has such a kind bedside manner."

"Your cousin was my teacher at J.T. Moore."

I enjoy any passing conversation that starts with, "You don't know me, but I knew your...," because even if you've lived in the same place most of your life, sometimes it takes a total stranger to fill in the missing pieces of your family puzzle.

Nowhere have I learned this lesson more than with discovering the life of my Uncle Larry, who died in a car accident before I was born. When my son, Matt, started school, he made friends with a boy named Tyler. Two years later my daughter Millie started school with Tyler's little sister, Margaret Anne. Their family took Matt and Millie on adventures to their grandfather's farm in Springfield, Tennessee.

The first time I met their grandfather, Carney Bell, he said, "I've got some stories to tell you about your uncle. You see, I was the medic who arrived at the scene of his accident." Carney was also the owner of the only funeral home in Springfield.

He and his wife had been friends of my uncle, who stopped by their place frequently for home-baked cookies and a visit.

Carney told me, "Your uncle was the kind of guy who would know all the names of the players on the other team before the ball game was over. Everyone liked him. Amy, on the day of Larry's funeral, the National Guard was called into Springfield to help direct traffic. Several of the streets were made one way to handle all the cars that came into town."

Years later I was playing golf at the Hermitage Golf Club when another player, a man named Ron Bargatze, pulled me aside and said, "Someday I'd like to take you to lunch and tell you about my childhood hero. His name was Larry Mayhugh."

Larry Mayhugh. He was the uncle I never knew. My sister Carol and I were born in 1959 and 1960 respectively, the years immediately following his death in 1958. As a child, my impression of him and of his impact on my mother, and consequently on our family, was extraordinary. A rare, gifted young man and amazing athlete, he was killed in a car accident during the spring of his senior year in high school. My mother must have been pregnant with Carol when she stood at the graveside, because my sister was born barely nine months later.

Growing up, I saw very few pictures of Uncle Larry. It wasn't until 1983 when I was cataloging some old home-movie footage with a projector that I could appreciate why. I had picked up a box of film from my mother's mother, whom we called Nanny. In hopes that the film contained rare images of my baby face (being the least photographed of the four of us as a typical lastborn), I finally figured out how to thread the machine and roll the film. Within seconds my enthusiasm and anticipation evaporated. The black-and-white image was three minutes of one long, continuous scan of flowers and funeral wreaths. They stretched from one end of the horizon to the other. No one had ever described this scene to me before, but I knew it was Larry's funeral.

In fact, no one had described very much about Larry at all. Oh, I knew a few passing details, like when he was a kid, his feet smelled so bad that he had to leave his shoes on the front porch all night. I knew he was a tease and had scared Nanny and my mom one day when he poured ketchup all over himself and lay crumpled on the kitchen floor until they came in and nearly had heart attacks. I knew he loved my mother and called her Deanie. But that's about it.

I remember one particular night when I was eight or nine years old, Carol and I stayed up late talking in Carol's bed. We talked about Larry, what little we knew about him. We had heard he used to take our sisters, Kathy and Mimi, to the locker room after his basketball and football games. I guess we worked ourselves into tears on our mother's behalf. Why didn't she talk about him more? We knew she missed him. We missed him, and we had never even known him. I remember that at some point Mom came upstairs and comforted us. I can't remember what she said, but I do recall she steered the conversation away from the subject of her brother.

My curiosity has only grown the older I've gotten. In the last years of Nanny's life, she lived in the country with my sister Mimi and her family next door to my family. One day I asked her what it was like to have a son whom it seemed the whole world was watching. What did it feel like sitting in the stands of his games, being the mother of the hero?

Now, I loved my grandmother. She was animated, beautiful, and fun loving—a real looker. I watched her gaze drift as her mind looked back across the years. And then she said, "Amy, I had the sharpest cape, luxurious material with a fur-lined hood." She must have been describing an outfit she had worn at one of Larry's football games, not the details I was hoping for.

But maybe I understood a little better why my mother kept her memories of her brother to herself. Maybe the two women in his life were not good at grieving together, so they grieved alone. I never even saw my uncle's grave until we buried my grandmother beside him in Springfield, Tennessee, on December 30, 1992. The holly tree that had been planted by his headstone decades earlier was full of red berries. I don't know how many times my mother had been out there over the years, but I had never seen the place, not until that warm winter day when we laid my grandmother to rest beside him.

I've heard that five years is the average marker for some semblance of normalcy following a tragedy. Five years after a divorce, five years after an accident, five years after a death—the present reality, the new reality, has a chance to stand on its own without being overshadowed by the past. My early childhood years were grieving/healing years for my mother. I can say this, not because she ever said so herself, but because now that I'm in my late forties, I've done enough grieving and healing myself to understand the process.

Over the years, I've pieced together the impact of Larry's death and how it has reverberated through generations. The details of my mother's child-hood are sketchy. My grandmother, Lura Kate Logan, married Robert Edward Lee Napier when she was sixteen. Many years after I was married, I asked my grandmother what it was like to be married so young. How had she handled a sexual relationship when she was barely old enough to experience desire or sexual impulses? She described crawling into bed and wrapping her nightgown between her legs, pretending to be asleep. Nanny made it all sound so funny, describing it as an old woman looking back. One thing is sure—when she married, she was a kid.

Two years later she had my mother. When my mother was two and a half, Nanny and my grandfather divorced, unheard of at that time in 1933. Consequently, my mother was sent to live with one of her twelve aunts and uncles on a farm. Aunt Thursey and Uncle Charlie were quiet, hard-working people, and my mother stayed with them almost five years. When Lura came back to pick up her daughter, she brought with her a new husband and a step-brother. By the time my mother was nine, Robert Napier, my mother's father and the link to her beloved Napier grandparents, had died. On the bright side, my grandmother gave birth to a son, James Larry Mayhugh.

My mother adored Larry, and everyone knew that the feeling was mutual. Unlike my petite mother, Larry grew tall like an oak tree. By the time he was in the second grade, he was using a chair and desk from the eighth-grade classroom. By the time he was in eighth grade, he was starting on the high-school varsity football squad. He was redshirted his freshman year so he could play out the rest of his high-school career. When my grandmother was in the last years of her life, I made a scrapbook out of Larry's newspaper clippings and the letters he received from coaches across the Southeastern Conference (I'm ashamed to say that I ruined several of them in my attempt to preserve them in clear, sticky paper). More than building a scrapbook, I was trying to connect to the boy in the pictures, the man who would have been my only uncle. Slowly the pieces of the puzzle have come together. Not all of the emotion of it. Not the vibrant colors of firsthand experience, but an evolving understanding of the family landscape into which I was born, its horizon stretching into the present.

Just a few months ago, my parents had a gathering at their home as part of the garden club my mother enjoys. During a casual conversation, one of the guests mentioned that he had been an assistant coach at Vanderbilt University for part of his career. My mother asked him if by chance he remembered a player who was scheduled to play in the fall of 1958, a young man who was killed before his graduation from high school.

When my mother said her brother's name, this man's face lit up, and he launched into a conversation that lasted most of the evening. They looked at old pictures and an MVP trophy Larry was given at the Clinic Bowl. The gentleman remembered watching my uncle play.

"Gloria, Larry *was* the franchise. That's why everybody in the SEC wanted him. You know why he chose Vanderbilt, don't you? He wanted to be near his family."

Larry had asked his sister's advice on his decision. My mom had said, "If you choose Vanderbilt, we will be in the stands." Now Mom and Dad both teared up recounting the conversation. What a gift that man gave to my mother!

I love Frederick Buechner's words in his essay on remembering: "For as long as you remember me, I am never entirely lost." Just because a life is cut short doesn't mean it can't provide a lifetime of impact for those still living.

I WILL REMEMBER YOU

I will be walking one day
Down a street far away
And see a face in the crowd and smile
Knowing how you made me laugh
Hearing sweet echoes of you from the past
I will remember you.

Look in my eyes while you're near
Tell me what's happening here
See that I don't want to say good-bye.
Our love is frozen in time
I'll be your champion and you will be mine
I will remember you.

Later on
When this fire is an ember
Later on
When the night's not so tender
Given time
Though it's hard to remember darlin'
I will be holding
I'll still be holding to you
I will remember you.

So many years come and gone
And yet the memory is strong
One word we never could learn
Good-bye
True love is frozen in time
I'll be your champion and you will be mine
I will remember you.
So please remember
I will remember you.

Shovel in Hand

Life can change in the blink of an eye
You don't know when and you don't know why
"Forever young" is a big fat lie
For the one who lives and the one who dies

I watched my son — shovel in hand
Go from bulletproof boy to a full-grown man
The cool dark dirt on the casket lands
Nineteen years old and he's buryin' a friend
Goodbye two boys, hello one man

This son of mine will leave in the fall
New friends might ask why he stands so tall
His life was changed with a telephone call
Not even he understands it all

I watched my son — shovel in hand
Go from bulletproof boy to a broken man
The cool dark dirt on the casket lands
Nineteen years old and he's buryin' a friend
Goodbye two boys, hello one man

I watched my son — shovel in hand
Go from bulletproof boy to a full-grown man

—May 15, 2007

Missing You

SONGS CAN HAVE MULTIPLE INSPIRATIONS. One of the inspirations for "Missing You" came from my sister Mimi's experience of sending her oldest son, my nephew Logan, to college.

Up till that point in time, my mom and dad, all three of my sisters, their husbands, and all of our children—fifteen between us—had lived in Nashville. An "immediate family" dinner meant twenty-five places had to be set.

When Logan packed his things and drove off to Sewanee, Tennessee, we all knew it was the end of an era. The next year Grant and Burton would leave, then Grace, then Caroline, then little Mimi...and on and on. The years we were all together in one place were precious. It was sad to see the beginning of the end.

But life goes on, and tears dry. We eventually stopped asking Mimi how she was doing.

One morning in late October, she was standing in my kitchen having a cup of coffee. Out of the blue and quite nonchalantly, Mimi mentioned that she'd bought a longer cord for her bedroom telephone. (These were before pocket-sized cell-phone days.)

"That way if I'm taking a bath, I can pull the phone all the way to the tub. I'd hate to miss his call," she said.

That one comment spoke volumes.

This part of life, the letting-go time, seemed like a million miles away from me and my three little ones. But like every younger sibling does, I watched my sister making her way through this process, knowing my time would come.

MISSING YOU

Your smile lights up a room
Like a candle in the dark
Warms me through and through
And I guess that I had dreamed
We would never be apart
But that dream did not come true

And missing you is just a part of living
Missing you feels like a way of life
I'm living out the life that I've been given
But baby I still wish you were mine

I cannot hear the telephone
Jangle on the wall
And not feel a hopeful thrill
And I cannot help but smile
At any news of you at all
I guess I always will

'Cause missing you is just a part of living
And missing you feels like a way of life
I'm living out the life that I've been given
But baby I still wish you were mine

My Sisters

My sisters are mothers and daughters
 Secret keepers and problem solvers
 Knitters and skywatchers
 Stillness and safe harbors

My sisters are table setters and providers
 Truth tellers and writers
 Laughers and criers
 News spreaders and tear driers

My sisters are porch sitters and coffee drinkers
 Average cooks and average cleaners
 Pillow fluffers and soul healers
 Confidantes and true believers

Aunt Jean

STORIES CIRCULATE THROUGH A BIG FAMILY like the messages in the children's game Operator, repeated again and again until they evolve into something very different from how they started. It's not always appropriate to ask the questions necessary to separate the truth from the embellishments. The exaggerated details and funny stories become part of the person and the story, every bit as important as the truth.

My great-aunt Jean was the seventh child of a seventh child of a seventh child of a seventh child. She was Grandmother Grant's youngest sister, eight years older than my father, and the closest thing to a sibling he ever had. In my eyes she was as distinctive and magical as her place in the family tree. As soon as she could, she left Tennessee, religion, and her southern roots and headed to California. She only came back for special occasions like weddings, funerals, and her mother's birthdays.

Some people make you feel more alive in their presence—who knows why. Aunt Jean had this effect; she was an old soul with a fresh smile for those she loved. She was beautiful in a rugged, tomboy sort of way, with thick, short hair, twinkling eyes, and a mischievous smile. My dad told me she had been a good athlete, a decent golfer and tennis player. We all knew she had a quirky sense of humor—when Jean was younger, she guarded a pet hair that grew out of her upper arm.

I loved that she was different. She was always easy to talk to, but she never talked about God. At times in her life, she drank too much. I guess she lived with some ghosts back in California, but I never felt their presence when she came to Tennessee. I remember her phone calls to our house when I was in middle school; hearing her voice on the other end of the line, I'd hope Mom would pick up on another extension and rescue me from an hour-long conversation. She always did. Mom loved Jean. I did too, but I was just a kid and too young to appreciate family ties just yet.

I never knew the love of Jean's life, but I had heard he died in a plane crash in the middle of the night flying military maneuvers over the desert just six weeks after their wedding. My cousins, Chuck and Trish, were products of her second marriage. I got to know them on their trips to Nashville to see Great Mimi, and when they would pass through town on their way to North Carolina to visit their dad and his people. Jean and the cousins' father, Charles, must not have stayed together long. I never knew him.

When I was twelve, my grandmother took my sisters and me to Santa Barbara for my cousin Trish's wedding. I'd never been to Aunt Jean's side of the country. Her house was in the mountains and had a distant view of the ocean. The terrain was rugged and dusty, the trees tall and magnificent. I'd never seen such displays of fruit as I saw on the roadside stands near her house.

One afternoon as I was prowling around her kitchen, I decided to help out unasked. Unloading the dishwasher is not easy in a strange house, and I was just finishing the job when Jean walked in.

"Honey," she said in her lazy southern drawl that she never lost, "that was so kind of you. Next time why don't we run the washer before we empty it." She must have been a heavy rinser. Still, she left the dishes in the cabinets, at least in front of me. And that has stuck with me.

When I started singing and writing songs, Aunt Jean was a constant voice of encouragement. She told me my songs broke down the old walls against religion she had built up. I told her I wasn't big on religion myself, but that I had faith in Jesus. She came to my first concert at Lakeside Amusement Park in Denver, Colorado. She came to my first Los Angeles appearance at Hollywood High School and took me to the Brown Derby afterward for a celebration dinner. "Everyone famous eats here," she said. Jean came to Knott's Berry Farm to hear me sing at a Christian music festival, probably the closest thing to church she'd been to in years. She and my cousin Trish and some more family watched uneasily as an overzealous threesome found out I'd never spoken in tongues. There by the side of the stage they grabbed my chin and neck and head and started praying at full volume that the Spirit of God would fall on me. I kept sneaking peeks at Aunt Jean, anxiously wishing the prayer would end.

In the spring of 1990, Jean was diagnosed with acute leukemia. My dad said the prognosis wasn't good. She braved all the treatments and sported her dandelion wisps of hair and failing body with her customary dry wit and ease. Through her illness, she had a lot of time to process her life and her relationship with Trish. That was a good thing.

Two times in the last month of her life, I flew to California to be with Jean and Trish, once with my sister Carol, the last trip with my sister Mimi. My daughter Sarah was six months old and made both trips. We went through boxes of pictures and mementos and took our time talking through old memories. I opened one box, and bits of ash fluttered out. I touched the singed wallet, the charred effects, graphic reminders of the love she had lost. For the first time, Jean told me about waking up in the night long after Frank should have been home, waiting in the dark for the phone call that came at daybreak.

On one of our last nights together, Carol, baby Sarah, Trish, Jean, and I lay up in her bed together like a pack of yard dogs, breathing each other's breath, talking and being quiet. In a few days, Sarah would be seven months old. In a few weeks, Jean would turn seventy.

"Amy, I'd like you to sing at my service," she said. "That would mean a lot to me."

"What if I start to cry?" I said. "What if my throat tightens up and I can't sing at all?"

"Well, honey, then just wait for that moment to pass," she said, "and when it does, then keep on going."

Jean died on her seventieth birthday, April 30, 1993. I sang the song I had written for her, starting and stopping and starting again like she told me to.

OH TENNESSEE

Oh Tennessee, I'm coming home to the ones who love me
This time around it's bittersweet
Oh Tennessee, you've been the cradle of my own dear family
Gently won't you rock my soul to sleep

Oh Tennessee, I'm coming home on the arms that hold me
Sweet Jesus' love is strong enough to save me
I'm letting go of everything that's been hanging on me
And plunging deep beneath the healing flood

And I wonder when I'll see his face or a chariot of fire
I wonder if I'll run on streets of gold
I'll see the One I've heard about since I was just a child
But I'd like to say one thing before I go...

Oh Tennessee, the trees in bloom—they come and go too soon
And this life of mine—it happens just the same
I'm heading on and in my heart I'll keep the memories of
The ones who share my love and share my name

Dad

DURING THE RECORDING OF *Legacy*—a collection of hymns from my child-hood—I invited a group of old friends I had gone to church with when I was younger to come to the studio and sing congregational-style background vocals on the old song "Marching to Zion."

Some of us hadn't seen each other in years. We were laughing and shouting and rehearsing while the clock was ticking and the studio bill was adding up.

To settle the group down and focus our attention on the job at hand, I asked my dad to lead us in a prayer.

Vince, Brown, and Steve Bishir, the engineer, were all in the control room, overseeing the recording. On hearing my request, Vince called out to Steve, "Hit the Record button."

With lyric sheets rattling in the background, my father's words were cap-tured by the computer.

A few days later, I sat down at the sound console to okay the final mix of "Marching to Zion." Brown and Vince spoke a quick disclaimer about the opening sound quality, but they said they hoped I would see the purpose in it.

Expecting bagpipes to come droning out of the speakers, I was surprised to hear shuffling paper...and then my father's voice.

Lord, You've blessed us so much with friendships that have lasted all
these years. We give you thanks for that.

We want to blend the output from these friendships into a message about you in a song that will be pleasing to you and will reach out to the world, to other people.

Bless this time, Lord.

Bless these efforts.

We praise you in Jesus' name.

Amen.

All of us were choked up as we listened to his words. Brown and Vince, both having lost their dads, said, "Trust us. Someday you'll be so glad you have his voice here to listen to."

Months after the CD was released, the engineer's wife, Traci, was tucking their six-year-old daughter, Sterling, into bed. When it was time to thank God for the day, Sterling launched into a prayer that was staggeringly eloquent. Not until the child spoke the phrase "Bless these efforts" did Traci recognize my father's prayer and that her daughter was quoting it verbatim.

Of course, I've known for a lifetime that his example is a good one to follow.

True Love

VINCE AND I WERE DRIVING IN THE CAR a couple of years ago, and I was spilling my guts out to him about a topic I can't remember now. He was quiet—listening, I hoped.

Eventually he made a comment or two that made me feel as though he fully understood me, maybe even more than I understood myself.

In the quiet that followed, I studied his profile. I was filled with gratitude and relief that here in my forties I was experiencing what I had dreamed of and longed for since I was a young woman. I tried to find the words to communicate my wonder in being fully understood by a man.

Finally he said with a smile, "Amy, I don't want to take credit where it isn't due. I love you, but I can't say I always understand you. What I can say is that I welcome you. I welcome you, and whatever you bring to the table is enough."

I thought, *Better still.*

TRUE LOVE

No one ever told me
During all those lonely tears I cried
That someday you would hold me
I just kept hoping inside
That true love was waiting
That true love would find me in time
That true love was waiting
That your love would finally be mine

No one ever showed me
Such care and tenderness
Darlin' you know me
And what moves me the best
It's true love—waiting
True love, making up for lost time
True love waiting
Your love, that's finally mine

I can't erase these lines on my face
I'd turn back time if I could
But all the years wanting, the desperate longing
Is maybe what makes it so good
True love waiting
True love that found us in time
True love waiting
Your love that's finally mine

Lead Me On

Lead me on
To a place where the river runs
Into your keeping...

LEAD ME ON

Shoulder to the wheel
For someone else's selfish gain
Here there is no choosing
Working the clay
Wearing their anger like a ball and chain
Fire in the field
Underneath a blazing sun
But soon the sun was faded
And freedom was a song
I heard them singing when the day was done
Singing to the holy one

Lead me on
Lead me on
To a place where the river runs
Into your keeping
Lead me on
Lead me on
The awaited deliverance
Comforts the seeking...lead on

Waiting for the train
Labeled with a golden star
Heavy hearted boarding
Whispers in the dark
"Where are we going—is it very far?"
Bitter cold terrain

Echoes of a slamming door
Chambers made for sleeping
Forever
Voices like thunder in a mighty roar
Crying to the Lord

Lead me on
Lead me on
To a place where the river runs
Into your keeping
Lead me on
Lead me on
The awaited deliverance
Comforts the seeking...lead on

Man hurts man
Time and time again
And we drown in the wake of our power
Somebody tell me why

Lead me on
Lead me on
To a place where the river runs
Into your keeping
Lead me on
Lead me on
The awaited deliverance
Comforts the seeking...lead on

Moonlight Conversation

Sometimes I crave a kind of connection with nature, with myself, with God that I don't know how to achieve. The absence of it makes me feel caged up inside. I can't sit still. I can't listen well.

The other day I felt this way and talked of going to the farm. I planned to ride horses, go on a hike, sit on a hillside. As it turned out, by the time I pulled out of the driveway, heading for the country, carrying two dogs, two kids, and pulling a tent camper, the sun was an hour from setting. There wasn't enough daylight left to do anything. So I just positioned the camper on the edge of the woods and left it there.

I turned on lights in the cabin, and left the girls to listen to their latest obsession, *High School Musical.*

I alternately pulled weeds from between the wooden porch steps and sat in the rocking chair, then pulled more weeds, then rocked a little...all the time wondering, *Is this it?* Was this moment the thing that had made me so antsy to leave town? Now I was antsy in the country, and getting bug bites.

At least the girls were having fun, singing soundalike lyrics at the top of their lungs, not much of it making sense, but that didn't matter to them.

By now a butter yellow moon had risen over the treetops, and I was compelled to walk through a little stacked-rail fence onto the open hillside where Vince and I had said our wedding vows. The beauty of the sky at night and the stillness of the warm summer air were beginning to settle in on me, and I could feel their calming effect. The pacing in my mind and heart was slowing down.

And as I stood there, gratitude began rising to the surface.

Gratitude for so many things… For this time in my family's history, marriages, babies, for my parents, for all the comings and goings under my own roof. This uncluttered, uninterrupted moment with my bare feet on the grass made me feel closer to the connectedness I longed for.

Maybe I should pray. Maybe out loud.

But when I opened my mouth, the words seemed outside the moment. My voice too thin. The actual sounds inadequate and out of place.

If this had been male-female communication, words would have stopped and touch would begin. How natural. But how does the created connect with the Creator?

I welcomed my gratitude, pictured my loved ones, and then began moving my arms, my hands, my feet in communication… I saw my sisters' faces. And then I bent down, reaching, and then stood, stretching up, and I rocked my arms and my body and pictured all of us rocking each other's babies…

And then I was marching and seeing my father, and dancing a jig... And then I moved in gratitude for my mother, kneeling, and bending, and rising... And then for my children and Vince, and I moved and twirled and danced, and balanced, and stood and spun until I was panting and my heart was racing...

And I felt connected.

Later, walking back to the cabin, it occurred to me that I should do a little more stretching to stay limber so I can pray wordlessly in the moonlight when I'm ninety.

ANGELS

"Take this man to prison," the man heard Herod say,
And then four squads of soldiers came and carried him away.
Chained up between two watchmen, Peter tried to sleep,
But beyond the walls an endless prayer was lifting for his keep.
Then a light cut through the darkness of a lonely prison cell,
And the chains that bound the man of God just opened up
        and fell,
And running to his people before the break of day,
There was only one thing on his mind, only one thing to say:

Angels watching over me, every move I make,
Angels watching over me!
Angels watching over me, every step I take,
Angels watching over me!

God only knows the times my life was threatened just today.
A reckless car ran out of gas before it ran my way.
Near misses all around me, accidents unknown,
Though I never see with human eyes the hands that lead me home.
But I know they're all around me all day and through the night.
When the enemy is closing in, I know sometimes they fight
To keep my feet from falling, I'll never turn away.
If you're asking what's protecting me then you're gonna hear
        me say:

Got his angels watching over me, every move I make,
Angels watching over me!
Angels watching over me, every step I take,
Angels watching over me...

Though I never see with human eyes the hands that lead me home,

Angels watching over me, every move I make,
Angels watching over me!
Angels watching over me, every step I take,
Angels watching over me!

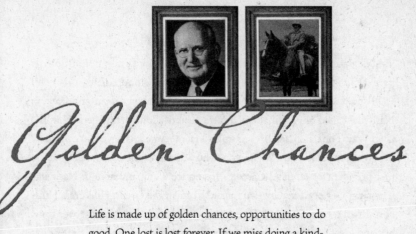

Golden Chances

> Life is made up of golden chances, opportunities to do good. One lost is lost forever. If we miss doing a kindness to a friend, we can never do that kindness again. If we might speak a pleasant word, or offer a bit of worthwhile counsel or advice and fail to do so, we can never have just that opportunity again. Giving is a way of life.
>
> A. M. BURTON (1879–1966)

THE BEAUTY OF BEING IN THE MIDDLE of life is the vantage point it provides. From my forties I can look ahead to my parents navigating old age at full tilt and take mental notes about what lies ahead. Even from here I can see that growing old is not for the cowardly. At the same time I can look back to childhood and the young-adult years with more understanding and compassion for myself in retrospect, for my children, and for all the young people I know who are swept up in the swirl of the early decades of life.

Finding one's way, learning to value the truth as a nonnegotiable plumb line, experiencing the consequences of violating the laws of nature or the laws of the Spirit, exercising free will, and realizing one's own impact on and in the world—these are all included in the sometimes painful lessons of life, and most of these must be learned firsthand. Thankfully, though, some principles can be inherited. I hope to pass on to my children a few very important lifestyle patterns that were established for me by my family, not just by my parents and my grandparents but also by my great-grandparents.

For a few years of my childhood, my family lived on a dead-end street in Nashville called Shy's Hill, named for a famous Confederate general in the Civil War. The land itself backed up to a farm named Seven Hills, owned by my great-grandfather, A. M. Burton, who was one of the cofounders and the first president of Life and Casualty Insurance Company here in Nashville. The farm was bordered by two major streets in the Green Hills area: Hillsboro Road to the west, and Tyne Boulevard to the south. Slowly, over time, bits and pieces of the farm were sold off or given away, until the time of my childhood, when my great-grandmother was in the last two decades of her life. All of her descendants, my great-aunts and great-uncles, second and third cousins, were enjoying the remaining acres of her beautiful countryside home on borrowed time.

You see, Great Mimi and Granddad had decided to will their entire estate to David Lipscomb, a Christian university in Nashville. Even as a child, I knew the details of their will because it was a matter of frequent conversation amongst all of us, their descendants. In the end, whether a cousin agreed or disagreed, whether a grandchild raised eyebrows or shrugged, the decision remained firm. The gift had been promised.

This generosity toward people outside our family circle taught me a couple of valuable lessons early on. First, people are free to do whatever they want with the things they've worked hard to attain. Second, with blessing comes a responsibility. With great blessing comes great responsibility. My great-grandparents understood the responsibility of caring for their neighbor, and their neighbor was not just their blood relative. This attitude also spared our family from the threat of greed that sometimes accompanies dividing a large inheritance. The question, *How much will I get when she dies?* never even tickled the edges of my brain. I already knew the answer: nothing. My inheritance from Great Mimi and Granddad was a daybed that held sleepover memories from my childhood.

Over and over, this principle has been reinforced throughout my life. Not long after Great Mimi died, a friend told me that if I would learn to give money away when my income was small, then the pattern would be established. If lots of money ever started coming in, I would already be accustomed to passing it around. Like Granddad wrote, it would become "a way of life." In a letter he wrote to his co-workers he said,

> The life which gives multiplies itself; the life which absorbs destroys itself and others. All nature is built upon the plan of giving. The sun gives its light and heat, the bird its song, the lilac its odor, the orchard yields its fruit for the good of man, the field its grain for the same purpose. If a man is not a giver, he is out of harmony with his surroundings. If he makes a dead sea of himself, he becomes fatal to anything that seeks life from him.

My attitude and approach to giving cannot be separated from how I view God and, consequently, my fellow man. *Do I believe in God? Do I believe that my needs are met by God? And if he can supply my needs, what about everybody else's?*

I remember a friend of mine telling a story about one of his first paying jobs. When he was in seminary, he and his wife pastored a small church in a rough part of Houston. They lived in the parsonage and received a salary of one hundred dollars a week. One day a college friend of his passed through town and stopped by for a visit. The friend's career was in sales, and at the time, 1972, he was doing quite well, with a six-figure salary. He said to the young pastor, "You were pretty sharp in school. You know, you could be doing a lot better financially if you had chosen a different profession. For instance, if you were with my company, you could be making a hundred thousand dollars a year."

My friend eyed his buddy and said, "Well, I don't know if I could live on that."

"What do you mean, you don't know if you could live on that? You don't look like you're making half that much now."

My friend said, "Well, I don't right now, but I work for someone who promised to pay me whatever I need. This last year I didn't need much, but what if next year I needed more? I sure would be in a mess if all I had was a hundred thousand dollars."

This is trust: doing what you believe you are called to do and trusting that God will provide. But here's where it gets personal: God provides through people. Am I willing to be connected to the people in my world, the people at work, the people in my house, the people I encounter in everyday patterns of living? Am I open to the possibility of my life, my gifts, touching another life? My life touching another, the domino effect of God's goodness rippling through so many other lives, is a powerful, far-reaching concept.

An older friend of mine gives away her bonus check every year, and she asks me to help find a good use for the money. She explains it to me this way: "Amy, you see more need firsthand than I do. You can find the needs that I don't see. Put this money to good use."

It took me a few years to understand the lesson for me in this challenge. Then one day I was having a conversation with another woman I have known since childhood. She confided in me that if she had the money, she would create a bank account just for benevolence, a store of money to be given to people who love and serve God and the people around them, and never see any reward for it. Laughing, she said, "What fun it would be to be God's delivery girl."

I thought about the annual bonus check from my friend. In the past, I had put the money to good use by donating it to major charities. But now I felt like I had a more personal way to honor the request: "Amy, find the needs that I can't see."

This year I signed the check over to the bank as an account to be administered by "God's delivery girl." Very soon I started hearing my friend's excited stories of how God was providing for people's needs through this fund.

- Money for much-needed clothing was given to a young wife and mother.
- A hard-working schoolteacher found her unexpected hospital bills covered.
- A minimum-wage employee was provided emergency car-repair money.

Could the answer to all the needs of the world be met if we would simply listen to the still, quiet voice of God, the voice that speaks to the universe, prompting us toward one another?

All around us are opportunities to give. To give what? Money? Money is only a small part of what is needed in the world. You cannot give what you do not have, but everyone is wealthy in some way. We can give support, encouragement, advice, attention, praise, honor, blood, respect, time, energy. Each of us is gifted in unique ways, and our generosity springs from those wells.

I think about Phyllis, who has helped me raise my children for the last twenty years. Every time I get on a stage, every time I'm doing an interview, every time I board a plane to do publicity, Phyllis holds down the fort. We have a common purpose, to raise these children in a loving, meaningful, respectful way. Phyllis has so many gifts—decorating, storytelling, helping—and she consistently gives out of her own abundance in those areas.

My daughter Millie's gift is writing and organization. My brother-in-law Jack has a brilliant mind, and he's great with numbers.

My gifts lie elsewhere. Ask me about planning an evening of music, and my mind turns and churns with energy. Others are gifted with athletic ability, people skills, or kindness. All of us have different strengths, and there are people all around us who need what we have to give. When one person is in need, another person has the opportunity to reach out and help.

Last Sunday I was rushing through the grocery store, trying to restock our empty refrigerator. We had been out of the basics for two days—eggs, milk, juice, dog food. I wanted to be on time to meet Vince at the airport, and I could see my window of time for getting it all done closing.

My cell phone rang. Gina was on the line.

"Hey, girl, what are you doing?"

"Panicking." I explained my time crunch.

"I'm in the neighborhood; why don't I meet you at the checkout and run your groceries home so you can go on to the airport?"

It was a simple act of giving, but it changed my whole day.

It's this exchange of caring and being cared for that is full of dignity and joy for both sides. Both lives are expanded. Both people are empowered with hope for a better way. Both experience a connectedness to each other.

Giving never happens by accident; it's always intentional. The apostle Paul says, "Remember this: Whoever sows sparingly will also reap sparingly, and whoever sows generously will also reap generously. Each man should give what he has decided in his heart to give, not reluctantly or under compulsion, for God loves a cheerful giver" (2 Corinthians 9:6–7).

All of us want our lives to be meaningful. The answer to that longing will never be found in a bigger flat-screen television, a new wardrobe, the perfect figure, or a bigger house. The secret to a life well lived is in giving. When we give, our lives are touched and changed.

HELPING HAND

Everybody needs a helping hand
Take a look at your fellow man
And tell me what can I do today
'Cause everybody needs a helping out
If that ain't what it's all about
Tell me what, what can I do
What can I do today?

We've all seen trouble from time to time
There's a mountain ahead
I've got no strength to climb
If you're feeling that you're strong
Reach out to me
I hope this journey won't take long
But won't you please
Have mercy

'Cause everybody needs a helping hand
Take a look at your fellow man
And tell me what can I do today
'Cause everybody needs a helping out
If that ain't what it's all about
Tell me what, what can I do
What can I do today?

I'm talking 'bout the soul all alone
Needing the daily bread
Someplace to lay his head
And I'm talking about the neighbor on your street
Won't you look him in the eye
Take time to speak
That's mercy

'Cause everybody needs a helping hand
Take a look at your fellow man
And tell me what can I do today
'Cause everybody needs a helping out
If that ain't what it's all about
Tell me what, what can I do
What can I do today?

Love one another, sister and brother
Love is the only way

Following

I'VE NEVER BEEN A GOOD FOLLOWER—not in traffic, because I have poor eyesight; not on the dance floor, because I don't relax enough; not with directives, because I like to find my own pace and my own expression. My mother asked me once if I felt that God was leading me in a tangible way. Did I feel that I was following a path marked out by him? On the contrary, I pictured myself like a milkweed in the wind, blown about until the breeze finally settles. I want to be led, but I am not a good follower. So how does a freewheeling, creative-thinking person absorb an invitation like the one Jesus spoke, "Take up your cross and follow me"?

I remember making a plan on a Sunday morning years ago for our family to visit a new church. My children were young—Sarah still in diapers. Being on time is a challenge for some of us, and even more so when small children are part of the picture. This particular morning I had left us a good safety margin of time, but one thing led to another, and everything started backfiring. Sarah was fed, dressed, and ready. While I was checking on Matt and Millie, Sarah got ahold of a slice of toast with grape jelly. By the time I found her, the dress had to go. A wet towel took care of sticky hands. The problem with outfit number two was sudden diarrhea. A wet towel was not going to fix this one. After a bath and outfit number three, I finally got us to the car. As I was struggling with the straps of the car seat (a struggle made more difficult by her stiff body—I'd be mad, too, if I had been dressed and redressed three times in a hurry), I imagined that this might resemble God's experience with me. He knows where he wants to take me, and he'll get me there, in spite of myself.

Moved

MY MOTHER-IN-LAW, JERENE, and I were having a cup of coffee one morning, and she asked me to name my five life-changing moments. She had seen a television show about the pivotal moments in a person's life, and she was curious about mine. I began scrolling through four-plus decades of both highly anticipated and unexpected experiences. Giving birth...taking risks...discovering a career path. Certainly meeting Vince and connecting with him in such a profound way at such an unexpected time was life changing. What else would I include?

I thought about our conversation for days. I realized that for better or worse, many of our pivotal experiences are hard to talk about. For years I have been too shy (or afraid of sounding like a nutcase) to describe one such experience in my life, but certainly it changed me forever.

When I was in my early thirties, I went with my sister Kathy to hear a man speak at a church down on Music Row in Nashville. At that time in my life, I found myself frequently in the company of sick children. The Make-a-Wish Foundation would call me to host a sick child backstage at a concert or make a hospital visit or a phone call to a terminally ill teenager. Sometimes families would come to our farm, and we'd spend the day together: riding four-wheelers, playing music, watching the sunset, talking about life and about death. I have already outlived most of those children, but if there could have been a different outcome to their lives...that is why I went to this conference to hear Jack Deere.

I hadn't heard him speak before, nor have I heard him speak since that day fifteen years ago. He had been a seminary professor and was now an author. Basically his teaching was a biblical perspective on healing: the circumstances and accompanying dynamics, the presence of compassion, the purpose to glorify God. It was an intelligent and insightful seminar, not accompanied by the emotional outpouring that sometimes goes along with such teaching. At one point during his talk, Jack invited any of us who were interested in the gift of healing to come down to the platform. Kathy and I were sitting in the balcony. I told her my hands were sweating a little bit, but that I wanted to go down front.

I don't remember any familiar faces in the crowd of about seventy-five people who streamed down to the front of the church with me. I stood toward the outside, hemmed in by several people, and listened as we were led as a group in this simple prayer: "God, all that you have for me, I receive."

I'd never prayed a prayer like that. I cupped my hands in front of me, callused fingertips on my left hand, no nail polish. Thoughts about food, about my growling stomach, came to mind. *Not now... Not now... A cheeseburger sure sounds good... Refocus...*

"All that you have for me, I receive." I rolled the whispered words around on my tongue, unfamiliar up until that moment. I was not asking for anything, which was different.

Then my hands moved.

No longer cupped side by side, they were several inches apart from each other. I was more than a little surprised. And how ironic—here I was at a healing seminar, willing to be used in any way, in a miraculous move of the Spirit of God, and yet I found myself completely dumbfounded by a ten-inch shift of perfectly functioning hands.

Okay, okay, stop fixating on the hands. Just say the prayer. And I did.

"God, all that you have for me, I receive."

These and only these words were formed by my silent lips, but my mind was like a wandering four-year-old's. *Man, am I hungry... Did I move my own hands?... Definitely not... What just happened? Oh yes, the prayer.*

"God, all that you have for me, I receive. All that you have for me, I receive."

The next time my hands moved, they took my arms with them, gently bumping the person to my right. Not acceptable behavior for any southern woman bred with manners. I turned a quarter turn so as not to disturb anyone else. My mind was racing. *No bumping allowed. Who is moving my arms?*

I was full of amazement and wonder. I even tried tugging my arms down a little bit. They popped back up. Three more times my hands moved, until they were completely stretched out over my head, my body taking the X position of a jumping jack. I was starting to smile and felt I could laugh out loud if I let myself.

My eyes had been closed up to this point. I was afraid that if I looked at anyone else or saw anyone looking at me, my self-consciousness would get in the way of whatever was going on. Finally I craned my head around to find Kathy in the balcony. I was trying to say with my facial expression, *Either the whole world is about to get healed, or I'm about to fly across the auditorium like a bird.*

And then the meeting was over, and I was laughing and hungry and changed.

1974

We were young, and none of us knew quite what to say,
But the feeling moved among us in silence anyway.
Slowly we had made quite a change
Somewhere we had crossed a big line.
Down upon our knees,
We had tasted holy wine,
And no one could sway us in a lifetime.

Purer than the sky,
Behind the rain.
    Falling down all around us,
    Calling out from a boundless love.
Love had lit a fire;
We were the flame.
    Burning into the darkness,
    Shining out from inside us.

Not a word, no one had to say we were changed.
And nothing else we lived through would ever be the same,
Knowing the truth
That we had gained.

Purer than the sky,
Behind the rain.
　　Falling down all around us,
　　Calling out from a boundless love.
Love had lit a fire;
We were the flame.
　　Burning into the darkness,
　　Shining out from inside us.

Stay with me, make it ever new
So time will not undo, as the years go by,
How I need to see
That's still me.

Purer than the sky,
Behind the rain.
　　Falling down all around us,
　　Calling out from a boundless love.
Love had lit a fire;
We were the flame.
　　Burning into the darkness,
　　Shining out from inside us.

The Brazos River

THE AIR TEMPERATURE IN THE EIGHT-SEATER prop plane must have been over one hundred degrees. We never gained enough altitude to cool down the cabin, so we sweated and baked for the hour-long flight from Houston to Mineral Wells, Texas.

By the time we touched down, we were wringing wet, and Vince, carrying Corrina, literally fell out of the plane into the arms of our old friend Dudley Hall. He and his wife, Betsy, had invited us to come to their ranch for a few days of rest.

Dudley's always been an outdoorsman, and Vince loves to fish, so we spent our time skeet shooting, fishing, and playing on the banks of the Brazos River. Corrina—water bug that she is—would have stayed in that river from morning till night. I couldn't blame her. The river runs wide and shallow through a canyon and isn't much more than thigh deep most of the way across—except near the far bank where it finally drops off. Corrina loved wading out to the middle of the river, looking for fish, splashing, simply enjoying the pleasure of it all.

Everything about that river is timeless. Not one house or power line can be seen from the water's edge. I thought about the first travelers passing through this hot part of Texas—how the wide, cool, slow-moving river must have quenched a deep thirst—a thirst in the throat, and a thirst in the eyes for the sight of such beauty. Dudley said that the whole name of the river is

Rio de los Brazos de Dios—"The River of the Arms of God." A good name.
A sacred place.

I couldn't help feeling a little wistful watching Corrina in all of her innocent beauty playing in that water. More in thought than in prayer, I looked
at the Brazos, longing to be able to wade into it and have the muddy water
wash away all the shackles that I felt...all the chains that weighed me
down...the weight of all the decisions I'd made in my life.

I'm not saying I wanted to be anywhere else. I was grateful to be at this
place in life surrounded by the ones I love—to lie down at the end of the day
in peace beside my heart's partner. It was just that I'd grown accustomed to
the ache of grief caused by life, by loss, by doors closed that can never be
reopened, the ripple effect of my choices. Consciously or unconsciously I had
incorporated scars and shadows into my emotional movement the same way
a war veteran accepts a permanent limp or a disfigured limb—just glad to
still be alive.

But standing on the banks of that river, I felt heaviness and longing, a
wistful ache.

The morning we were leaving, Vince and I were packing our bags and
talking. Out of the blue he said, "What do you think about having Dudley
baptize Corrina in the Brazos River?" Between late-night card games and cups
of cowboy coffee sipped around our morning campfire, Dudley had been
steadily reminding us about grace and mercy. When Vince mentioned a bap-
tism, it thrilled me. It also made me think that, at three years old, Corrina was
not old enough to have made this decision for herself. Instead, I suggested that
we go to the river and dedicate her to God.

That day had dawned clearer than any other during our stay, and after
breakfast we headed for the river. Dudley and Vince, Corrina and I, walked
into the water. Under a crystal-clear blue sky, breathing the sweetest air I'd
breathed in a long time, Dudley spoke to us and prayed for us and for our
daughter, who seemed even more precious to us because of the promise we
were making.

As we were collecting ourselves to go back up the hill, Dudley piped up and said, "Hey, does anybody here want to be baptized?" At those words my heart began pounding like a jackhammer.

"Are you kidding?" I said.

"No," he said, "I don't have a plan or an agenda. I'm just offering since we're here and we've got the water."

Everything in me was rushing…my thoughts…my heartbeat…my breath. I said yes.

I'd been baptized on a Sunday night in May of 1973, the spring of my seventh-grade year. After our church service, I was on my way to a youth dance at my next-door neighbor's church. Straight hair was in at the time, and I'd painstakingly ironed my hair that afternoon, not knowing that I'd be walking the aisle at the 6 p.m. service.

As silly as it sounds, even as I was celebrating being forever transferred from the kingdom of darkness to the kingdom of light—I was also a little anxious about how my hair would survive the baptismal cap.

Nothing was the same at forty-three. Dudley and I waded across the expanse of that river heading for deeper waters…all forty-three years of me…three decades of life lived since the Sunday night that young woman walked the aisle. Years of pleasure and pain…of child bearing and growing…of birthdays and funerals…of lessons learned and innocence lost. I walked into that water carrying *everything* with me.

Dudley called out to Vince, "Hey, Vince, do you want to be baptized too?" And Vince answered with a phrase I've heard him say a hundred times, "No, Dudley, I'm just here to support my bride."

I wish I could remember what Dudley prayed as we stood there. All I can say is that his words spoke to every wounded, broken place in me. I felt as vulnerable and as known as I have ever felt. And as he pushed me under the surface of the river, all the weight of grief and pain washed downstream. The prayer I didn't even realize I had been desperately praying for such a long time was now answered.

Mosaic

When I came up out of the water, the air was buzzing as if electrified. The sky was alive, undulating with a thousand shades of blue. All of nature was singing. I was awestruck with the newness. Amazed. Loved. Clean.

And I turned to Vince to see if he could see what I was seeing, hear what I was hearing. Instead what I saw then was my precious friend quickly pulling off his T-shirt and his ball cap and wading into the deep waters with us.

Vince and I were baptized in the Brazos River on June 15, 2004.

THE WATER

Quicksand, my heart is sinking
I try to run but I can't stop thinking
I'm climbing walls, I'm on the ceiling
It's gonna take a miracle to heal me

I'm staring down into the quarry
I see a stone for every sorry
I'm on the edge, I'm going under
And after I die I'm gonna rise from the water

I want to blast off,
Let gravity disappear
I'm tired of falling, falling, falling
From the weight of fear
Come and lift me up
Into the clean and clear
I'm waiting on you Jesus in the water here
So come and wash me clean

The sky is red, there's blood on my hands
I can't deny, I'm guilty where I stand
The verdict's in, I hear 'em shoutin'
Send me a river to drown this mountain

Mosaic

I want to blast off,
Let gravity disappear
I'm tired of falling, falling, falling
From the weight of fear
Come and lift me up
Into the clean and clear
I'm waiting on you Jesus in the water here
So come and wash me clean

Breath of Heaven

"BREATH OF HEAVEN" WAS A COMPLETED SONG when Chris Eaton first played it for me—a beautiful worship song. At the time I was in the process of collecting material for a Christmas album. Haunted by his melody and the lyrics of the chorus, I made a very presumptuous and probably somewhat rude request. I asked Chris if I could rewrite the three verses to make "Breath of Heaven" a Christmas song.

Imagining the experience of the Virgin Mary as she traveled to Bethlehem was made a little easier by my own pregnancy with my daughter, Sarah. I was almost seven months along when I recorded the vocal track. In fact, the night that I recorded "Breath of Heaven" we were having a family gathering with all the Chapman relatives. I asked my sisters-in-law, Sharry and Carole, to come back to the studio with me after dinner. I knew that if I could sing to them about Mary's experience, then I would feel less self-conscious about the recording process and more energized to communicate the soul of the song.

Brown Bannister, my dear friend who produced that record, filled the studio with candlelight. The mood was expectant and vulnerable. Shane Keister played the piano. We recorded our parts simultaneously. Listening to each other breathe, we felt our way through the dynamics of this beautiful song.

BREATH OF HEAVEN
(MARY'S SONG)

I have traveled many moonless nights,
Cold and weary with a babe inside,
And I wonder what I've done.
Holy Father you have come,
And chosen me now to carry your Son.

I am waiting in a silent prayer.
I am frightened by the load I bear.
In a world as cold as stone,
Must I walk this path alone?
Be with me now.
Be with me now.

Breath of Heaven,
Hold me together,
Be forever near me,
Breath of Heaven.
Breath of Heaven,
Lighten my darkness,
Pour over me your holiness,
For you are holy.
Breath of Heaven.

Do you wonder as you watch my face,
If a wiser one should have had my place?
But I offer all I am
For the mercy of your plan.
Help me be strong.
Help me be.
Help me.

Breath of Heaven,
Hold me together,
Be forever near me,
Breath of Heaven.
Breath of Heaven,
Lighten my darkness,
Pour over me your holiness,
For you are holy.
Breath of Heaven.

First Thing

MORNING COMES TOO EARLY. Most days the third ring of the alarm finally pulls me out of bed. Like every other working mom, I hit the ground running—checking off the list formulated in my head as I lay falling asleep the night before. I've tried for years to figure out a way to start my day off on the right foot. Many people have told me to make my first conscious thoughts ones toward God. Others have encouraged me to have Bible study before the day gets started. The problem is that I simply forget. My good intentions have never become workable habits. I guess we all have to find what works for our unique wiring in our own lives. Somewhere in this last year I came up with a rhythm that has stuck.

When I wake up in the morning—regardless of the temperature, whether the sun is shining or the rain is pouring—I go outside. I speak aloud to the predawn darkness or the tail end of the moon just kissing the edge of the horizon or the 9 a.m. bright sun of a sleep-in Saturday morning. I say, "This is the day that the Lord has made. I will rejoice and be glad in it." I say it out loud because I'm groggy. I say it out loud because I'm speaking it and hearing it. And I don't just say it once.

As the cobwebs and sleepy confusion start lifting from my brain, I keep saying that phrase, accenting different syllables, placing varying degrees of importance on different words. "*This* is the day that the Lord has made." *This*—the one I'm in right now. Not yesterday. As much as I want to reach back and relive something or reminisce or bring back somebody who's gone

143

or feel what I once felt—that's all in the past. I can't reach it, I can't touch it, I can't return to it even if I tried. The door is closed. *This* day—the one I'm standing in—is the day the Lord has made. *This* is the day. *This* is it. How I live this day is what matters.

"This is the day that the Lord has made." If God made this day, if he intended for me to wake up this day, then there's a purpose in it. It wasn't made because he was bored and had nothing better to do. He created it because that's his nature—he is creative. And he creates for his pleasure. And here I am right in the middle of a creation that was provided for his pleasure. Where do I fit? How am I a part of it? These questions start turning in my head.

"*I will rejoice* and be glad in it." I've got several choices ahead of me. I can worry. I can fear. I can hesitate. I can plan. I can be regretful. But these first words out of my mouth—*I will rejoice*—remind me that this, too, is an option. I have the option to choose rejoicing and to be glad.

As I speak, I feel my senses waking up. I hear the chatter of the birds. I smell the air. I feel the wetness from the dew on my feet. This is my early-morning meditation. If "wake-up speed" could be measured like car speed, optimal being zero to sixty in three and a half seconds, I'm probably zero to twenty-five in fifteen minutes. But this initiative on my part is doable, even in my sleep-drunk stupor. I can go outside because I love the outdoors. I can throw a blanket over my shoulders. I can survive out there without my contacts, without shoes. In whatever mental state I might happen to be, I can greet the day and engage my spirit for the hours ahead.

Like everybody else, I wish I were in better shape or had planned an upcoming event a little more thoroughly. I wish I were neater. I wish I weighed what I weighed when I was in my thirties. But all those things are for another day. *This* day—at a hundred and forty-five pounds, at forty-six years old, with a few gray hairs and not quite enough sleep—*this* is the day the Lord has made. *I will rejoice* and be glad in it.

On the heels of my wake-up call, I say the Lord's Prayer, slowly, deliberately. When Jesus came to earth, he revolutionized our accessibility to God, so it only makes sense to follow his advice when he said, "When you pray, pray like this."

"Our Father who art in heaven."

Our Father. All of us, everyone who's ever lived or died—we share him. We are his. Whether we are lovable or unlovable, whether we agree or disagree, saint or reprobate—all of us have the same Father, our Father who art in heaven.

"Hallowed be thy name."

Holy. Set apart. The Great Other. I can't even say "Hallowed be thy name" without thinking of all the times in the course of a day when I inadvertently say, "Oh my God." This is my time to say, "I'm sorry for throwing your name around."

"Thy kingdom come. Thy will be done."

What do I know about God's kingdom? The first shall be last, the greatest is the servant of all. Whoever loses his life for Jesus' sake will find it. This all seems upside down to me. Here my prayer becomes, "Help me see my world the way you do, to look at the heart and not the exterior."

"Thy will be done, on earth as it is in heaven."

I can assume that at any given moment what's happening in heaven is exactly what God wants to be happening. But here on earth, with all of us roaming around with our loads of free will, we have the option of saying either, "I think today I'll just be about what I want to do," or, "Thy kingdom come. Thy will be done." It makes me take a deep breath and consider my to-do list, the things that I find important, the ways that I plan to invest myself.

By myself, all I have is my own knowledge, my own experience, my own vantage point. How narrow. If I am on an eternal time line with things of eternal significance happening all around me, why would I want to be confined by my limited perspective? How much better to speak these words:

"Thy kingdom come. Thy will be done, on earth as it is in heaven. Let me be a part of your plan. I'd rather not be limited to just my own."

"Give us this day our daily bread."

My daily bread. Whatever I need this day. God sees it better than I can. Maybe my daily bread includes rest, maybe peace, patience, direction, creativity, work, wisdom. Even more, he can see what I don't need, the things I wander after, the things that swallow up the hours and leave me empty. "Whatever you know that I need today, I'm asking you for it."

"Forgive us our debts, as we forgive our debtors."

This sounds like a black-and-white equation. Forgive me the way I forgive. Yikes. Is Jesus teaching me a lesson even in the prayer he taught me to pray?

What do I feel I'm owed? Where have I invested myself with no return? From whom do I honestly believe that I deserve an apology or a thank you? What tally sheet am I hanging on to? Can I react to any expectation—anything that I think I'm owed—with the same ocean of mercy that's been poured over me? I need grace to see the entire debt that I have been forgiven, so that I can extend that same mercy to someone else. Burn the tally sheet. Mercy doesn't keep score. "I forgive my debtors. Thank you for forgiving me."

"And lead us not into temptation, but deliver us from evil."

I don't understand the mystery of how God works, but I pray how Jesus told me to. "Lead us not into temptation. Don't take me somewhere that's dangerous for me. Don't give me what I'm asking for if I can't handle it."

"Deliver us from evil."

I think about a baby being delivered—pushing and shoving and womb walls squeezing in. Then it is delivered into the hands of a waiting family. Is that how we are delivered from evil? Am I coming through this world pushed in on every side, and it's messy and crazy and sometimes looks as much like death as life? "Deliver us from evil. Find us safe passage. See me safely through."

"For thine is the kingdom, and the power, and the glory forever."

All of this is God's. It's his to rule. He alone is capable of finishing this thing he started. "God, you deserve endless gratitude and celebration from all your creation. Thank you. Thank you. Thank you."

Amen.

Takes a Little Time

It takes a little time sometimes
To get your feet back on the ground...

Takes a Little Time

It takes a little time sometimes
To get your feet back on the ground
It takes a little time sometimes
To get the Titanic turned back around
It takes a little time sometimes
But baby you're not going down
It takes more than you've got right now
Give it time

What's this walking thru' my door
I know I've seen the look before
Sometimes on faces in the street
And sometimes in the mirror looking back at me
You can't fix this pain with money
You can't rush a weary soul
You can't sweep it under the rug, now honey
But it don't take a lot to know

It takes a little time sometimes
To get your feet back on the ground
It takes a little time sometimes
To get the Titanic turned back around
It takes a little time sometimes
But baby you're not going down
It takes more than you've got right now
Give it time

Now it may not be over by morning
But Rome wasn't built in a day
You can name that thing a thousand times
But it won't make it go away
Let me put my arms around you
And hold you while you weep
We've been talking and talking and
I'm sick of this talk
And it's nothing that won't keep
It takes a little time...

This, Too, Shall Pass

These familiar words are a good reminder that nothing stays
the same, even if you want it to. And, thankfully, especially when
you don't.

My brother-in-law Jerry asked me to inscribe that saying on a piece
of leather years ago (my first job was leather crafting with my
friends Helene and Nolan). I was a teenager then, and I remember
carefully cutting and hammering those words onto a strip of
cowhide and hand tooling it into a bookmark.

This, too, shall pass.

As I write the phrase now, my mind is scrolling through endless
images of my life—family dinners with my great-grandparents, the
old neighborhood I grew up in, a thousand music performances,
moments with my children—so tender that I feel as if my heart is
being squeezed inside my chest, moments I would freeze in time if
I could.

This, too, shall pass.

My old friend Billy's fiancée was killed in a car wreck on a road trip.
That man grieved like the world was coming to an end—shaved off
his beautiful curls and hid away from everyone and everything till
he could see straight. Later he said, "Sometimes the greatest act of
faith we can muster is just putting shoes on in the morning."

This, too, shall pass.

Billy married sometime later, when there was a little gray in his hair, and became a dad too.

Nothing is wasted in life. Grief and pain enlarge our capacity for compassion and perseverance.

Good times, well, they speak for themselves.

Seashells and Anita

VINCE AND I WERE RECENTLY IN CABO SAN LUCAS, Mexico, for a children's hospital foundation fund-raiser. On the dining-room table of our *casita* sat a large bowl filled with enormous seashells—giant conchs, nautiluses, sand dollars, and whelks. My mind drifted back to childhood summer days and late-afternoon beach walks with Anita Johnston, AJ, the woman who vacationed in the condo above ours on Lido Beach in Sarasota, Florida. I cannot count the hours I spent in ankle-deep tide pools searching for seashells and occasionally looking up to the same view—pockets of dimply, swinging skin on the backs of her thighs—both of us leaning over, our fingertips skimming the surface of the water.

A native of Nashville and the fifty-something-year-old mother of four loud, colorful kids, Anita loved to talk, and I loved to listen. She talked to me as if I were an adult, even though I was probably in the fifth or sixth grade when we were at the height of our shell-collecting glory. She talked about people, God, and her children, and about her heart, which had always been weak. Congestive heart failure, she called it.

If she was sick, you'd never have known it from the way she lived her life. She was gregarious and passionate, opinionated and sometimes exasperated. And I got to hear it all. She had a quick and easy laugh, high cheekbone, and a beautiful mouth. She loved the sun, the water, and the sand, and I loved watching the wind in her reckless gray-streaked curls. Her pleasure was palpable as we moved down the beach and around the point in our meandering fashion.

"You know I'm going to die, Amy. I keep telling everyone, and nobody's listening. When they least expect it, my heart is going to give out." I kept a watchful eye on the bent figure in front of me, just in case she keeled over during our shell hunt. But she remained healthy for many summers and was always glad to see me, eager to share the latest treasures she'd found since we were last together.

Years later she did die, a lot earlier than her friends. She'd left funeral instructions and hidden notes all over her house for her four grown children to find after she was gone. I was away and couldn't attend the service, but I learned that at her request she was buried in her clown costume, the one she had worn on numerous visits to the children's hospital. This wasn't a surprise to me, because she talked a lot about her funeral all those years before, during our saunters down the beach.

The beach in Sarasota has gone through a lot of changes. As with every great getaway spot, developers are hungry to maximize the potential of the real estate. The ocean is still beautiful, but long stretches of endless sand have been replaced by wall-to-wall high-rises. In the spring of 1998, I took my children back to the beach I had known so well as a child. At that time, our home life was eroding. Spring break was being split between their dad and me. I get a knot in my stomach even now thinking about how lost and hopeless we all felt back then.

On our last morning there I took a walk by myself down the southern stretch of beach. The ocean had eaten away so much of the sand that there was no way to get around any of the old condominiums without swimming. But the day was too gray and cold to attempt such a feat. I walked where I could, just the short distance leading up to the wall of an old building that stuck out into the surf. This was the only walkable piece of my old treasure-hunting ground. The sand was coarse and dirty, not fine and delicate. There were no tide pools, just crudely crushed shells left in gray lumpy mounds.

Barefoot, I had to pick my way over the crunchy, gravel-like surface. *What happened to this place? Doesn't anything stay the same?*

It didn't take long to reach the retaining wall, and then it was time to turn back. Back to what? You can't go back; you can't go back to an old beach; you can't go back in time; you can't go back to innocence. You can't go back anywhere, can you? Life keeps chugging and churning. Left in the wake, I felt like one of those shards of old shell—unrecognizable, uncomfortable, ugly. What I wanted was to be whole. I wanted my children not to be broken. I wanted us not to feel like these shells. I even said that out loud to the biting wind. Is there any hope of feeling whole again after life has left you churned up?

At that very moment I looked down and saw just in front of my toes one perfectly whole, delicate sand dollar the size of a nickel. I was amazed. Out of habit I'd kept my eye on the ground as I'd been walking, but up till now hadn't seen even a piece of a shell any bigger than a matchstick head. As I bent to pick up the sand dollar, I caught sight of a miniature whelk, a rare treasure to find even when I was a kid. Immediately beyond that shell was a prince's slipper. I'd collected hundreds on my walks years ago. And then I saw a turkey wing and then a sunset shell. And finally the rarest one of all, a tiger's paw still connected to its other half.

I'd never seen one like that, not ever before. I could not believe that in two or three steps I had found the kinds of specimens that AJ and I would have considered the best of the best. I could picture her standing up tall and stretching the kinks out of her back as she lifted her smiling face to the clear sunset skies, holding the treasures up in the air.

I wrapped those shells in a tissue and later put them in a little cardboard box and wrote in marker on the cover, "Do not throw away." Almost a decade later when my parents decided to sell the beach place, someone found that taped-up box in the corner of a closet and returned it to me.

I rarely see a shell that I am not reminded of summer afternoons with AJ and of the hope I found on the beach.

ALL RIGHT

Looking out to the hills, to the setting sun,
I feel a cold wind bound to come;
Another change, another end I cannot see,
But your faithfulness to me

Is making it all right.
I fall down on my knees;
Tell me that it's all right.
You give me what I need.
Years of knockin' on heaven's door
Have taught me this, if nothing more,
That it's all right, what may come.

I've heard it said, when the river's running high,
You get to higher ground or you die.
Well, muddy waves of pain washed over me,
And it only made me see

It's gonna be all right.
I fall down on my knees;
Tell me that it's all right.
You give me what I need.
Years of knockin' on heaven's door
Have taught me this, if nothing more,
That it's all right, what may come.

When will I learn there are no guarantees?
What strengthens hope, my eyes have never seen,
But it won't be long
Till the faith will be sight,
And the heavens will say
It's all right
Whatever comes.

On Aging

It occurred to me this morning
    as I washed this face of mine,
How quickly come the changes
    with a little passing time.
A wrinkle here, a hair turned gray,
    a not so lilting step.
I see me growing older,
    but I don't quite feel it yet.
At times I nearly feel my age,
    at others I'm sixteen,
So full am I of all the thoughts
    and feelings in between.

Who would have thought the road of life
Would twist and turn so much?
The journey makes me strong and weak and
    tender to the touch.
And so this day I face the choice
    that I have faced each day,
Will I be open? Teachable?
Unafraid of change?
    Yes.

I will embrace this moment.
Forgive my past mistakes.
And remember that just showing up is
    sometimes all it takes.
I'll seek the kind of beauty
    that time cannot erase,
Wisdom and experience resting on my face.

I wrote the first half of this poem with my former husband, Gary Chapman, at the request of my mother. I finished it twenty years later with some firsthand experience.

The Deer

IN THE FALL OF 1989, A COUPLE OF FRIENDS and I took a much-needed road trip to a cabin in Indiana. We all had children at home. Two of us were pregnant at the time and looking forward to long, uninterrupted talks by the fire. After a good night's sleep, we put on the coffeepot first thing the next morning and started talking. By late afternoon, the conversation was still going, and we were still in our bathrobes.

All of us have life experiences that go untold. Maybe it was the safety of the cabin, the fact that the phone never rang, that allowed one of my friends to talk about her childhood so vulnerably. She told us a story that was sobering and terrifying.

I was seven months into my pregnancy, carrying my first daughter. Listening to this woman's story, I felt for the first time a very real fear for what might happen, what *could* happen, to my child despite all of my efforts to keep her safe.

A little bit of evil goes a long way.

A big dose is devastating.

We took a break in our conversation, emotionally drained. The sun would be setting soon, and we all needed a little space to digest everything that had been spoken. I showered and dressed and went outside. I wanted to yell at someone. I wanted to cry. Instead, I picked my way down the wooded hill and crossed a creek by crawling on my hands and knees over a fallen tree.

I could not make any sense of life, at least not of that woman's life. I wanted to stop imagining the details of her story. I couldn't.

As I reached the other side of the stream, I looked up and saw a deer standing in the trees about thirty feet away from me. It was not much bigger than a fawn, but old enough to have lost its spots. Slowly, I began walking toward the deer. He didn't run. When I was just a few feet away from him, I got down on my hands and knees and crept up beside him. I kept thinking he would bolt, but he stayed still.

Slowly I stretched out my hand until my fingers touched his nose. We both jumped back a little. Still he didn't run. I reached out again. This time I touched the fur on his neck…then his shoulder. I began petting him gently, then scratching his chest until I found myself wrapping my arms around his neck and leaning against him. It was the most peaceful interaction I have ever had with an untamed animal. After a while I backed away, turned, and walked toward the creek. When I looked back, the deer was gone.

It's hard to put into words what I drew from that unexpected experience. Strangely, a calm wonder had replaced my fear.

The next day, as we were packing to leave, the owner of the cabin dropped by to see us off. I asked her how long they had been feeding the deer around there. She thought about it a minute and said, "I can't say that I've ever seen a deer here before."

Jesus said, "Peace I leave with you; my peace I give you. Do not let your hearts be troubled and do not be afraid."

CARRY YOU

Lay down your burden
I will carry you
I will carry you, my child

Lay down your burden
I will carry you
I will carry you, my child

'Cause I can walk on water
Calm a restless sea
I've done a thousand things you've never done
And I'm weary watching
While you struggle on your own
Call my name, I'll come

Lay down your burden
I will carry you
I will carry you, my child

I give vision to the blind
And I can raise the dead
I've seen the darker side of hell
And I returned
I see these sleepless nights
And count every tear you cry
Some lessons hurt to learn

Lay down your burden
I will carry you
I will carry you, my child

Winter

It's interesting that so many of the great hymn writers battled depression. In fact, remarkable artists and leaders such as Picasso, Van Gogh, and Abraham Lincoln suffered from it as well. Winston Churchill called it the "black dog." Whenever I am in a bleak mental state, I think about these people whom I admire and realize that this condition is not unique to me.

The first time I remember feeling derailed by depression, I was nineteen, a sophomore in college. I dropped out of Furman University for the winter quarter. I didn't know to identify the dynamic as depression. I just understood it experientially, feeling like a piece of wood.

I've never seen the television show *Lost*, but I know the story line has to do with a group of people finding themselves in an unidentified place. They have to figure out where they are and survive until they can be found. Landing in the family gene pool can be a similar drama.

Depression runs in my family. My grandmother suffered from it. Years ago, my great-uncle told my cousin, "If you're born into our family, you have to start the day with a brisk walk." He knew the power of endorphins, even if he didn't know what to call them. Back in the early eighties, on a winter day in College Station, Texas, I wandered into a strip-mall pet store and found myself staring at a wall of fish tanks. The season of the black dog had me pretty well socked in, though I was still too young to understand it. I just remember watching the fish and churning on the inside, angry with them for their contentment.

Our understanding and treatment of depression has changed a lot since then. Antidepressant prescriptions are as common as birth-control pills. Except for a four-month period in 1999, I haven't relied on them. Probably my age and the circumstances of my life have softened the downward spirals for me, but winter is still a struggle every year. Maybe subconsciously that is part of the reason I've made so much Christmas music—to focus on hope and joy and store up a lot of good thoughts for the dark months ahead.

The truth is, I have a great life. I've made a career of my childhood hobby, and many doors have been opened to me. Still, I'm confronted with moods that just appear out of nowhere: feeling overwhelmed, feeling like what I have to offer is not enough, a deep sadness that is foreign to my usual optimism, loss of energy. In those times, it's hard to complete my thoughts, much less my sentences.

What I've learned so far is that depression can be, but is not necessarily, about circumstances or about a particular event. It is physical. It is hereditary. It is cyclical. Its onset is like traveling down a road and suddenly hitting a patch of deep sand, wheels spinning and no visible forward motion.

The good news is, I've learned to recognize it and not be ashamed of it. I know as surely as it comes, it will go. In the meantime, here's the talk I give myself:

- Don't be so hard on yourself.
- Simplify the to-do list.
- Be grateful for unavoidable responsibility. It makes you move.
- Be careful what you reach for.
- If necessary, be willing to say, "I'm having a hard time, and it's not you."
- My great-uncle Dandy was right. A brisk walk helps.
- Make contact with other people. Hear about somebody else's day.

Because I live with these occasional extremes in myself, I look at other people differently. We never really know what is going on inside another person. It's good reason to be gentle.

The Ride

She's acting crazy
running everywhere but home
telling everybody everything but the truth.
She thinks she's found the answer.
Finally someone sees her, loves her, understands her, and wants her.
She's empowered by the raw feeling.
She is reckless with the things she used to protect:

     her reputation

         her heart

             her children.

She lives for the phone to ring, for a glimpse of one car, for the sight
   of one face.

Where did she go? I see her, but she can't see me. It's as if she raised
this page close enough to touch her nose and cannot see anything
else. She only knows that she's going round and round and round on
the inside. This merry-go-round is an insidious ride. How did she
get here? Why now? Maybe she has had that ticket to ride burning
a hole in her pocket since she was a little girl. Maybe she doesn't
even know who put it there. We stand outside the guardrail calling
her name. She sees our faces in a blur each time she spins by again.

CRY A RIVER

Who knew love would come walking thru my door
Turn a light on somewhere down inside
And give me a feeling I'd never had before
It was a long wait
It was just the wrong time

But I hope you'll hold me now
Somewhere within
And when you think about
What might have been

Cry a river
Flood the sea
Cry a river over me
Take the bitter
With the sweet
And cry a river over me

How can you argue with a feeling in your bones
'Bout what is and what isn't meant to be
Some things you live with
And you never let it show
Like the pain I felt
The day I watched you leave

But I hope you'll think of me
When tender winds blow
Sit on the shores of love
And just let it go

Cry a river
Flood the sea
Cry a river over me
Take the bitter
With the sweet
And cry a river over me

Loss

Journal Entry
2003

The question is, "How do we live with loss?" The cycle of investment/loss is manifested time and again in our lives.

We invest in children. They grow up and move on.

We invest in partners, and eventually that familiarity is susceptible to some level of contempt. We invest in friendships, and circumstances change, needs change, and loyalties turn to lip service and loss.

Sometimes we're blindsided by it.

The ways I learn to deal with loss might be useful tools for my children. I must remember, "We mourn, but not as those without hope."

God's view of life, of us, is eternal. Loss is temporary.

SOMEWHERE DOWN THE ROAD

So much pain and no good reason why
You've cried until the tears run dry.
And nothing here can make you understand.
The one thing you held so dear, is slipping from your hands.

And you say
Why why why?
Does it go this way?
Why why why?
And all I can say is

Somewhere down the road,
There'll be answers to the questions
Somewhere down the road
Though we cannot see it now
Somewhere down the road
You will find mighty arms
Reaching for you
And they will hold the answers at the end of the road.

Yesterday I thought I'd seen it all
I thought I'd climbed the highest wall
But now I see that learning never ends.
And all I know to do is keep on walking
Walking 'round the bend.

Saying
Why why why?
Does it go this way?
Why why why?
And all I can say...all I know to say now is

Somewhere down the road,
There'll be answers to the questions
Somewhere down the road
Though we cannot see it now
Somewhere down the road
You will find mighty arms
Reaching for you
And they will hold the answers at the end of the road.

Don't Go

MY FRIEND RUTH HAD NOT BEEN FEELING WELL since her bout with the flu a few weeks earlier. She was one of the healthiest people I'd ever known. In fact, with three workouts a week for two solid years, she had, by becoming my personal trainer, single-handedly managed to pull me back from the brink of postpartum body hopelessness after my third child was born. Now thirteen years and many workout sessions later, she was feeling a little off kilter and not sure why. Her long, lanky, six-foot frame—did I mention no body fat?—couldn't hide the tumor for long. So she called the doctor, and he scheduled a complete hysterectomy.

Two days before D-day I drove to her house for a visit. I was leaving on a bus the night before her surgery, and I needed to see her face one more time during these days of anxious uncertainty. The thing she felt in her belly didn't have a name yet. Ruth stretched out on top of her white, old-fashioned bedspread. "Do you want to feel it?" she asked. She guided my hand to the area between her bellybutton and pubic bone. If I hadn't known better, I would have told her she was four months pregnant. "This wasn't here last week," she said. I closed my eyes and focused all my thoughts and energy toward my friend. "Do you mind if I pray for you?" I asked. "I would appreciate that," she said.

I said aloud my thoughts and intentions, my requests of God. I said aloud the things I believed about life and love and healing. I spoke ancient words of Scripture that have been spoken by millions in times of need—that our struggle in life is not against flesh and blood, but against the rulers, against the authorities, against the powers of this dark world. I spoke of our shield of faith, with which we can extinguish all the flaming arrows of the Evil One. I spoke about the beginning of all things, when the Word was with God and the Word was God. That through him all things were made and without him nothing was made that has been made. I prayed to the Life and Light of all people to illuminate this darkness, to bring peace, to bring healing. I prayed for God's mercy and his comfort, for the strength to receive all he had for us in this place.

Then I stretched out on the bed next to Ruth. Flat on our backs staring at the ceiling, we talked about the days ahead. She offered me all her tampons. "Guess I won't need those anymore."

I smiled. "At least the guesswork is gone about your trip through menopause." Recently I had gotten so mad at the sliding drawer on my DVD player that I had ripped it out of the machine. I had blamed it on an uncharacteristic rage, surely the result of a hormonal swing. Must be "the change." Ruth would roll into the operating room at one hormonal stage in life and roll out in the next. We reminisced about all the body changes we had seen each other go through over the years. All in all, that day was quite a gift, giving me the chance to tell Ruth the things I have loved so much about her.

Two days later on a Texas highway my cell phone rang and Ruth's husband, John, gently told me the findings of the surgery. "It doesn't look good," he said. "The doctors removed a large tumor, ovarian. The cancer has spread... They removed as much as they could... Enmeshed in her diaphragm... Won't know about the lungs... Stage three, maybe four..." I was trying to take it all in. White noise filled my head. "Now what do we do?" I asked John.

Calmly he said, "Amy, we give her as much support as we can to help her fight this thing. We can surround her with prayer and encouragement, with kindness, with good food, with fresh air. We can help her with the necessary tools she'll need, but in the end it will be a hard fight and a fight that she may not win. As much as we love her and want to be here for her, this is her journey, and it's a journey she must make. As long as she has the will to keep fighting, we'll help her fight. But if at some point she decides she's had enough, then we'll love her and support her until she dies."

I was so moved by John's quiet resolve. He would be a good partner for Ruth on this road. As for me, I hung up the phone, crawled into my bottom bunk on the bus, pulled the curtain shut, and sobbed in the darkness. I cried until I thought I was all cried out and then cried some more. I gritted my teeth and tightened my belly and growled my pain and grief, hidden by the steady roar of the bus engine. I thought my head would explode.

The last few hours of the drive to Farwell, Texas, were quiet. I felt weak and worn out and vulnerable. I wondered if Ruth was awake yet. I wondered how she would take the news. I guess this is what the next chapter looks like. Sure didn't see it coming, but the page on yesterday just turned, and now we're squarely on a new and foreign road.

Journal Entry
July 2006

Don't go.
Not yet.
Not while there is still so much to do.
I need your familiar conversation,
You are known by me and I by you.

Don't go.
Not yet.
I cannot hear you say we'll not make music on the hillside
When we are old and gray.

Or discuss our stretching skin or your gorgeous,
voluminous hair.
I so enjoy your regal face,
And the lines collecting there.

Don't go.
Not yet.
Not while there are still horses to ride
Words to say
Dogs to love
Melodies to play.
Timeless soul,
Friend of mine,
Though it is only to the other side,
Don't go.
Not yet.
Don't go.

A few months later I took a walk with Ruth. She had no hair and looked beat up, but she was winning the fight. "Amy, as awful as this has been, I'm so grateful for the gift of cancer. This experience of being weak, of having to receive help with basic daily functions, has made me grateful for every aspect of my life, even the hard stuff. I'm grateful for my family, for my health, and I'm especially grateful for every investment I've made in another person. If I could bottle this kind of appreciation and give it to you to drink, I would. I don't know if I have four months or four years or forty years—that's all right. The uncertainty of it makes every day a gift."

AFTER THE FIRE

After the fire is over
After the ashes cool
After the smoke has blown away
I will be here for you

After the stillness finds you
After the winds of change
All that is good and true between us
This will remain the same

Slowly, slowly
We turn the page of life
Growing, knowing
It comes at quite a price

After the fire is over
After the ashes cool
After the smoke has blown away
I will be here for you

After your time of wandering
Along this lonely road
There will be many voices calling
Mine will say welcome home

Mosaic

Slowly, slowly
We turn the page of life
Growing, knowing
It comes at quite a price

After the fire is over
After the ashes cool
After the smoke has blown away
I will be here for you
I will be here for you

Mother's Day

Mother's Day 2006 was cold in Nashville, unusual for May when climbing roses are already in full bloom. For a fire lover, the weather was a gift. I treated myself to two outdoor fires built in the copper fire pit that Deanna and Phyllis had given me for my birthday. My theme for the day was "I'm taking the day off." And I did.

By late afternoon I had settled myself outdoors in a rocking Adirondack chair in the backyard next to a roaring fire with a blanket over my legs, a good book on my lap, and a cool drink on the wide flat armrest of the chair.

I'd enjoyed the company of each of my children earlier in the day and was now enjoying the quiet, surrounded by my thoughts. Then the patio door opened and out walked Jenny, my twenty-four-year-old stepdaughter. She's always a welcome sight, but I had figured she'd made plans for the whole day with her mother. They are very close.

With a beautiful smile on her face, she called out, "I couldn't let Mother's Day go by without coming to see you too."

She joined me by the fire. As we sat there together, sipping from our glasses, catching up on the family news, my thoughts went back to the cloudy spring day Vince and I got married on a hillside in Williamson County. The pictures of our freshly blended family were filled with grim-faced children— Jenny was seventeen, Matt twelve, Millie ten, and Sarah seven. How many conflicting emotions were at work that day? All of us had been through several years of uncertainty and upheaval.

And then I scrolled back a little further to a fall afternoon six months before the wedding, to the first time I was ever alone with Jenny. We'd been at a golf course, watching her dad host a fund-raiser for Junior Golf at the Golf House of Tennessee. It was the fall of 1999, and Vince and I were in the first stages of being a public couple after several years of tabloid speculation. The day was beautiful and sunny, and Vince was obviously glad we were all in the same place at the same time.

For Jenny and me it was a different story. Our interaction was strained and polite. I remember looking at her face, watching her watch her father, feeling the unbridgeable chasm between us. I wondered how she felt about all the changes in her life throughout her high-school years. Now she was a senior, and her father had invited me into his world and consequently into hers. For some reason I thought about "We're Going on a Bear Hunt," a rhyme I had read to my children many times. In every refrain some obstacle presents itself, and the following chant echoes again and again:

> Can't go over it.
> Can't go under it.
> Can't go around it.
> Have to go through it.

I asked Jenny if she wanted to leave the golf course, hop in my car, and go to the Sonic Drive-In a few miles up the road. She shrugged and nodded and followed me to the car. I knew the conversation that needed to happen and was fighting back tears before we even got out of the driveway.

I felt like someone who'd borrowed a car without asking, returned it to the front driveway completely wrecked, then walked into the house trying to act like everything was normal.

It was an awful feeling.

Driving up Franklin Road, I found myself stringing thoughts and words together that I hoped she would hear. It took everything in me to push those words into the air between us.

In response, she rolled the window down and lit a cigarette. Then her cell phone rang.

I welcomed the chance to collect myself.

As I listened to her side of the conversation, it dawned on me that her life was filled with people whom she had chosen, as was mine. Circumstances had brought us together, but that didn't guarantee a relationship.

Slowly, awkwardly, we outlined a kind of truce between us: what she could tolerate, what we were willing to accept in each other. Even in this slightly adversarial setting, I loved her mind. It was a good first respectful step.

Over the years, little by little, meal by meal, birthday by birthday, phone call by phone call, Christmas by Christmas, card game by card game, trip by trip, movie by movie, conversation by conversation, we became family.

I had always wanted five kids.

Happy Mother's Day.

OUT IN THE OPEN

They were the sweetest words I'd ever heard
My heart could barely take it in
Like water offered to the lips
Of a tired and thirsty man
'Cause it's a tangled web I've woven
And I don't know all the reasons
But it amazes me to wake up
To your mercy every morning

So I'm standing here and spinning 'round
In the fields of freedom
And I'm still alive and reaching out
And I can feel the healing

When you say
Come on out come on out, out in the open
Come on out come on out, into the light
There is no jury
There is no judge
Ready and waiting
Are the steady arms of love

For the sake of never making waves
I kept my secrets to myself
And no one ever really knew
The darker shadows of my heart
But I will be a witness
That there's nothing in me dark enough
The power of forgiveness
Cannot rescue from the deep

So I'm standing here and spinning 'round
In the fields of freedom
And I'm still alive and reaching out
And I can feel the healing

When you say
Come on out come on out, out in the open
Come on out come on out, into the light
There is no jury
There is no judge
Ready and waiting
Are the steady arms of love

On children and faith

TODAY I DROVE OUT TO THE CABIN to write. First, I wandered around the hillside, guessing what the weather might do. I laid a fire in the wood-burning stove, just in case a cold front should blow in unexpectedly on this late-spring day. Then I put on a pot of coffee and scoured the Tupperware containers for snacks. The next hour I spent changing light bulbs, locating an extension cord, blowing up an air mattress, arranging quilts on it, and listening to a light drizzle on the tin roof above my head. I started working on a song. Then I noticed my cell-phone battery was dead. I decided to put it on the car charger and grab a Starbucks Double Shot out of the cooler to shake off the sleepy afternoon mellowness that had settled in on me.

On my way back to the cabin, I discovered a patch of late-blooming hybrid daffodils. I picked several stems and put them in my freshly rinsed Double Shot coffee can. These will look nice on my writing desk. On my way back to the car to retrieve my partially charged phone, I decided to restack the fieldstones around the outdoor fire pit. This was sweaty work and a little startling when the occasional lizard ran past my hands. Finally, with no urgent distractions left, I sat down and got to work. With my notebook and pen on the table in front of me, I began to write down what I had been thinking about all morning: children and faith.

> Train up a child in the way he should go, even when he is old he will
> not depart from it. (Proverbs 22:6, NASB)

Through the years, my most consistent prayer for my children has been, *God, find them the way you found me. Give them faith to believe you.* I've always hoped my children would discover the love of God in the context of our home, where we see the best and the worst of one another. At home they will see how we invest our lives, if we respond to the needs of others, if we serve, respect, accept, and forgive.

As I write this, our children are twenty-five, nineteen, seventeen, fourteen, and six years old. It's far too soon to tell what I've done right and what I've done wrong in passing on a heritage of faith to the next generation. Unlike my own childhood church routine—attending Sunday-morning services, Sunday-school classes, Sunday-night services, and Wednesday-night classes every week—my children have had a very sporadic church experience. Spending several months of each year on a tour bus when they were young contributed to this. When we were in town, we were involved in home-church settings, which was good for the adults, but less enlightening for the kids.

One night when my son, Matt, was young—maybe four and a half or five—he had a sore throat, and as I tucked him in bed he asked me to pray for him and I did. Expressions like "the faith of a child" came to my mind that night, and I smiled with wonder at his trust in God. The next morning Matt bounded into the room and energetically shouted, "That silly God! He didn't heal me!" He seemed cheerful enough in spite of the situation and ran out of the room as quickly as he'd run in. In that moment of quiet, I knelt by the bed and said a prayer. "God, I can't do a very good PR job for you if you don't show up. This is beyond my control. Just find him, please."

Then there were the rocky years. When I chose to end my marriage to the father of my three older children, there was a time when I was too wrecked and too ashamed to pray with them at night. Deep in my own crisis of faith, I didn't know how to reconcile our broken home with the picture of God I had tried so hard to communicate to them over the years. I had no answers to their questions or mine—questions like, "If God can do anything, then why didn't he fix our home?" And so, I was silent.

God, find me.

But it does take time. People come in and out of our lives at different times for different reasons. Responsibilities change, patterns change, interests change—we grow up and grow older. When I was a preteen in the early seventies, my two oldest sisters, Kathy and Mimi, starting attending Belmont Church, a very free-form, free-spirited, Bible-based congregation. Sometimes the old building on Sixteenth Avenue would be so full that people would have to sit cross legged in the aisles or perch in the deep sills of the stained-glass windows. I loved going into that place. I loved the singing. I loved the teaching. Life spilled out of those gatherings into many pockets of the Nashville community—the music scene, high society, school campuses, the lives of street people.

For those of us who had grown up with a lot of Bible teaching, the introduction of the Holy Spirit as an active and welcome participant in our church experience was exhilarating. Occasionally rumors flew around the conservative church world that our beloved pastor, Don Finto, was leading us into all sorts of debauchery. (I say that half kidding, although there were some interesting articles that hit the paper.) But the reality was that many Bible-believing people in that era had never been taught about the grace and mercy of God. The real work of Jesus. Forgiveness. It is not our good behavior that puts us in right standing with God. No one is that good. But instead it is believing in and receiving the work that Jesus did on the cross on our behalf.

Trust me, this good news blew the doors of celebration off the Belmont Church building. I thrived on that good news as a teenager. The vibrant knowledge of active mercy compelled me to write my first songs, to sing for anybody and everybody who would listen.

Years later in the wake of divorce, when the circumstances of my life had left me feeling like a stranger to myself and to God, an old friend from those early Belmont days showed up on my doorstep. It was late summer 1999. I was renting an amazing old house on Bowling Avenue. On this particular afternoon, Vince and I were playing Ping-Pong. Matt, Millie, and Sarah were at their dad's house. When the doorbell rang, I looked up to see a familiar face through the front window. The past was about to collide with the present. I shouted a quick explanation to Vince as I headed to the door: "Just picture Janis Joplin meets the last of the Jesus hippies!" And then Ginger walked back into my life.

I had not seen her in several years, but she was exactly the same as I remembered her. Ginger and her husband, Mark, had lived their entire married life on less than a shoestring budget and still found a way to give their time, their energy, and their money to spread the good news. They operated a grass-roots outreach to people in need. I guess I had become one of those people now.

This wasn't the first time one of them had intervened unexpectedly in my life.

When I was in college, I used to travel most weekends to sing, usually in churches. Sometimes I would leave school on a Friday morning, fly cross country, and play a show in Seattle that night, maybe one in Portland, Oregon, the next day. Then late Sunday I would fly back to school in time for classes on Monday.

One such weekend I had arrived at the Nashville airport without my purse. Of course, in 1980 no one needed an ID to pick up a prepaid airline ticket. This was long before 9/11 and long before airports had security checkpoints. But still, without a dime in my pocket, I was feeling scattered and unprepared to travel a thousand miles away. As I started up the one escalator that led to the departure gates in the old Nashville airport, I thought, *Oh well, it's too late now.*

Just as the concourse level glided into view, I caught sight of a familiar face with a long blond beard, waiting at the top. Mark Lang was standing there as if he'd been expecting me. "The Lord told me you were going to need this," he said, pressing a white paper into my hand as I ran for my flight. It wasn't until I got on the plane that I realized the paper was an envelope—holding thirty-six dollars.

I tend to be distrustful of the phrase "The Lord told me..." this or that. It's not that I think God is silent. I'm just wary of hidden agendas. But I do believe that God speaks to us through other people. I believe he had Mark waiting for me at the airport, just as surely as he sent Ginger to my house that day in 1999. The way she prayed was like an echo from my past. I was reminded that even though many things in my life had changed, some things never would, important things like God's mercy and forgiveness, and his power to find me.

That was eight years ago. This morning my youngest daughter, Corrina, grabbed my hand before school and said, "Mom, we forgot to greet the day!" I'd been awake for quite some time, had downed three cups of coffee, folded two loads of clothes from the dryer, made an earlier trip to school for Sarah's 7 a.m. track practice, and, yes, had greeted the day just as the sun was rising a few hours before.

"Okay, sweetie. We can do it on the way to the car. It's time for school."

"No," she insisted, "let's do it right now, out this door."

A few days earlier I'd shared morning prayers with Corrina for the first time. I didn't expect her to initiate the idea with me, especially on this Monday morning when we were all weary from the weekend. "Let me do it, Mom," she said.

She started with the words I'd used before: "This is the day that the Lord has made. I will rejoice and be glad in it. Good job, God! Good job on this day that you've given us. Good job!" Eyes slammed shut, she talked and prayed as openly and boldly as if she were chattering on to an old friend. As I listened to my youngest child pray, I realized, *He's finding her...apart from me. And she's responding to him.* They all are in their own ways. That's my prayer for my children, that when they feel the pull of God, they respond. That's my prayer for myself as well. Didn't God say, "You did not choose me, but I chose you"?

We ended our morning greeting with the Lord's Prayer. Corrina half said it, half shadowed me as I spoke the familiar words, "Thy kingdom come. Thy will be done, on earth as it is in heaven." *Thy will be done. What is your will, God?* And then I thought about Jesus' words, "For my Father's will is that everyone who looks to the Son and believes in him shall have eternal life, and I will raise him up at the last day" (John 6:40).

Whether we are aware of it or not, we pass on to our children the things that are important to us. It's in what we say and what we don't say, what we pursue and what we don't pursue, in what we value and what we don't value. In my parents' house, I learned to look at life in light of eternity. This kind of faith is what my parents passed on to me and what I hope to pass on to my children. In the end our children's journeys of faith will be as unique as our own. My prayer continues to be, *God, find them the way you found me.*

WHAT THE ANGELS SEE

If I could see what the angels see
Behind the walls, beneath the sea
Under the avalanche, through the trees
Gone would be the mystery
If I could see what the angels see

If I could hear what the angels hear
The thunderous crash of a falling tear
Holy holy in my ear
I'd never doubt that God is near
If I could hear what the angels hear

If I could know what the angels know
That death is just a swinging door
And spirits go where spirits go
I feel them but they never show
If I could know what the angels know

If I could stand where the angels stand
And watch the world while God commands
And see how love designed this plan
Reminders on his feet and hands
If I could stand where the angels stand

If I could see what the angels see
Behind the walls to you and me
And let the truth set me free
I would live life differently
If I could see what the angels see

The times of my life

YEARS AGO I WAS SEATED next to a stranger on an Atlanta-bound flight. I was a freshman in college at the time, on my way back to school after singing a couple of shows on the West Coast. I struck up a conversation with the young man seated next to me. Eventually he asked me my name. "Amy Grant," I said. "Amy Grant," he echoed thoughtfully, then repeated it again, trying to place the apparent familiarity. I sat quietly for a few moments and was just about to mention music and recording when a light came on, his face brightened, and he said, "Hey, I know you. You're the girl who is giving all those really bad haircuts at Furman University." I laughed, "Yeah, bad maybe, but at least they're free."

Along the same lines in the late nineties, I was in Sarasota, Florida, on a spring-break trip with my friends Bruce and Karen Moore. Bruce and I were waiting on the beach for the rest of our crew when a man and his grown kids came strolling up the sand. They looked at me for a minute, sort of hesitating, and then asked, "Would you mind taking a picture?" "Sure," I said, and quickly arranged all of us in a line, putting myself in the middle and motioning to Bruce to come snap the photo. Right about that time, the father said, "Actually, we were wondering if you would take a picture just of us." An understandable mistake on my part, but really embarrassing. Bruce has had a field day reminding me of that one ever since.

Lesson learned: Never assume anything about your own importance. It's a great big world, and all of us are busy living our lives. None of us knows all the time and effort that another person puts into his or her passion.

In an effort to provide a framework for some of the stories that I've shared in this book, I've jotted down a long, but certainly not exhaustive, music-and-life time line. This is just from memory and not meant to be a complete list of events or co-workers. My intent is to show how quickly I was set upon a path I did not anticipate and how that shaped my life. If I do not have a unique stage persona that differs from the me who shows up at the grocery store, it's because I've never felt any demarcation between life and art, faith and day-to-day living. Consequently, my family, my friends, and my work have always been entwined.

November 25, 1960—I was born in Augusta, Georgia, the youngest of four daughters of Gloria and Burton Grant. My family moved several times between Nashville and Houston before finally settling back in Tennessee with the rest of our extended family in the summer of 1967. One of my earliest musical memories was hearing my great-grandmother sing "How Great Thou Art" at Hillsboro Church of Christ.

1974—Started attending Belmont Church and had a life-changing youth group experience. Among the leaders were (fresh out of college) Mike Blanton, who would later become one of my career-long managers, and Brown Bannister, who would become the producer on most of my albums.

1975—I began playing guitar, a borrowed Martin D-35 (my sister Kathy's wedding gift to her husband, Dan Harrell).

January 1976—Wrote my first song, "Mountain Man," inspired by the movie *Jeremiah Johnson* and an old college roommate of my brother-in-law. My first audience: my mother.

Spring 1976—Performed in public for the first time as a sophomore at Harpeth Hall, an all-girls school in Nashville, with classmate Debbie Hogue. I had written about half the material and mixed my songs about faith with my favorite James Taylor, Carole King, and Elton John songs.

Late Summer 1976—Recorded a demo tape just for fun at Belmont College's recording studio with church friends Brown Bannister and Bill Lokey.

October 1976—Brown was dubbing a copy of my song tape at Goldmine, a basement recording studio in Brentwood, Tennessee. The owner, Chris Christian, a college friend of Brown's, heard the tape and called Word Records in Waco, Texas. Word was in the process of finding artists to launch a new contemporary-Christian music label. My tape was played over the phone, and I was offered a record deal, five weeks before my sixteenth birthday.

1977—Over spring of my junior year and fall of senior year, I casually and unhurriedly made my first record, produced by Brown Bannister, although he wasn't credited.

Spring 1978—My first album, *Amy Grant,* was released the month before my graduation from high school. I spent several weeks that summer on a promotional radio tour with my mother, covering the Midwest and West Coast.

Fall 1978—Drove to Greenville, South Carolina, to start my freshman year at Furman University.

September 21, 1978—Flew to Fort Worth, Texas, to see Brown and his family. Performed my first ticketed concert at Will Rogers Auditorium. The rest of my freshman year I was either flying from Greenville to Nashville to record or traveling to sing in a church.

May 1979—Released my second album, *My Father's Eyes*. Met Gary Chapman, the writer of the title track, at the album release party at O'Charley's in Nashville.

Fall 1979—My sophomore year at Furman saw more traveling. I dropped out of school for the winter quarter, spending a month in Switzerland at a retreat center called Edelweiss. While there, I received my first telegram: *My Father's Eyes* had been nominated for a Grammy Award.

February 1980—Still out of school, I recorded in Los Angeles for the first time, working with Brown Bannister and Jack Joseph Puig. I finally returned to Furman in March for spring quarter.

Summer 1980—My third record, *Never Alone*, was released (my worst-selling record). I collected a lot of air miles performing three to four shows a weekend with guitar player Gary Chapman and my brother-in-law/manager, Dan Harrell. He and Michael Blanton formed the management company Blanton/Harrell Entertainment, which continues to represent me today (now known as Blanton Harrell Cooke & Corzine).

Fall 1980—Transferred to Vanderbilt University. Played my first show with a band at Langford Auditorium on the school's campus. The band included Keith Thomas on piano and Dave and Dann Huff on drums and guitar, respectively.

January 1981—Between classes, I traveled to Memphis, Tennessee, to rehearse with the DeGarmo and Key band (a successful contemporary Christian rock group) in order to record a concert for a live record.

February 1981—Recorded two shows back to back at Oral Roberts University in Tulsa, Oklahoma, and OU in Norman, Oklahoma. Those were only my second and third experiences of singing with a band. The project was released as live records *Volume 1* and *Volume 2* a few months apart in the summer and fall of 1981.

Summer 1981—Between my junior and senior years at Vanderbilt, I toured the U.S. with the DeGarmo and Key band (much to their chagrin—very tough for those rockers to play "Giggle" every night), along with other members of the band: Billy Sprague, Dave Durham, Bonnie Keen, and Jan Harris. This was my first experience living on a tour bus. My friend and college roommate, Jeannie Cochran, was my road manager. Sometime during 1981, I met Michael W. Smith at the Paragon Publishing building. This dazzling West Virginia native became a dear friend, and his creative energy was a driving force in my songwriting.

Fall 1981—In late September of my senior year, I traveled to Caribou Ranch, situated just outside of Nederland, Colorado, for two weeks to record my next project, *Age to Age*. I turned twenty-one in November of that year.

Spring Break 1982—While my Kappa Alpha Theta sorority sisters went on a senior trip, I spent two weeks touring material from the yet-to-be-released *Age to Age* record. Great response. Included in the band were Gary Chapman, Michael W. Smith, Garrett (I can't remember your last name... sorry), John Goin, Mike Brignardello, Keith Edwards, Kathy Troccoli, and Janna Pastin.

May 1982—*Age to Age* is released. As my class graduates from Vanderbilt University, I sit in the crowd and cheer, twenty hours short of a diploma. At this point I realized my childhood hobby had become my career choice. However, my dad had made me promise that I would complete my college degree. Once in a blue moon he still asks me when I plan to finish.

June 19, 1982—I married Gary Chapman. Within the month we left for a six-week tour of England and Europe, performing as a duo to promote *Age to Age*.

Fall 1982—Launched my first major tour, singing five or six shows a week, touring the U.S., Canada, Australia, and New Zealand. The band included Gary Chapman, Michael W. Smith, Reed Arvin, James Hollihan, Mark Baldwin, Duncan Mullins, Keith Edwards, Donna McElroy, Kim Fleming, and Renee Garcia. *Age to Age* goes platinum.

April 1983—Returned to Caribou Ranch to record the basic tracks and vocals for the *Straight Ahead* record. Back on the road until July.

July 3 to August 23, 1983—Recorded a Christmas project in record time at several locations including Caribou Ranch, Nashville, Los Angeles, and London. *A Christmas Record* was released that fall.

Spring 1984—My eighth record, *Straight Ahead*, was released, attracting the attention of two mainstream record labels, A&M and Geffen. Tour schedule was extensive, covering U.S., Canada, Australia, New Zealand, and England. Included in the band were Gary Chapman, Michael W. Smith, Reed Arvin, Jerry McPherson, Tom Hemby, Keith Edwards, Donna McElroy, Kim Fleming, and Renee Garcia.

July 1984—Took a break from touring and made a fourth trip to Caribou Ranch to begin work on *Unguarded*. Ed Rosenblatt from Geffen Records joined us at Caribou. As soon as the record was completed, I went back on the road with the addition of Chaz Corzine as road manager.

August 10, 1984—John Huie became my booking agent and represents me to this day.

February 1985—First performance on the Grammy Awards, the song "Angels." Having watched Tina Turner strut around during "What's Love Got to Do with It" earlier in the show, I got cold feet about my high heels, and at the last minute, I pulled off my shoes and went barefoot. I must have made some kind of impression on Brandon Tartikoff, head of NBC at the time, because the next day he called Dan Harrell to book me for my own Christmas special.

Spring 1985—Released my ninth project, *Unguarded*. A&M Records was signed as the mainstream distributor for the new album. The single "Find a Way" made it into the pop Top 40. This album marked a change in direction for me. I remember the tension between honoring my Word Records contract, which called for explicitly Christian content, and my creative and spiritual need to create music with a broader subject appeal.

April 1985—Moved to Riverstone Farm in Franklin, Tennessee. A few months later, my sister Mimi and her family moved next door to us, much to my delight.

Spring 1985 to September 1986—I toured over 150 sellout shows for *Unguarded* across the U.S., Canada, England, Australia, and New Zealand, and performed for my single largest crowd in a day—forty thousand people. The *Unguarded* band included Gary Chapman, Reed Arvin, Phil Kristianson, Jerry McPherson, Tom Hemby, Tim Marsh, Keith Edwards, Donna McElroy, Kim Fleming, and Renee Garcia. During breaks in the tour, I recorded a duet with Peter Cetera, "Next Time I Fall," and filmed a video for the song. Returned from a tour down under to find that "Next Time I Fall" was number one on the pop charts.

February 11, 1986—I hired Deanna Hemby to be my personal assistant. She's still with me today.

Summer 1986—Recorded two new tracks, "Stay for Awhile" and "Love Can Do," to include with a "best of" release titled *Collection*.

November 1986—Filmed my first NBC Christmas special called *Home for the Holidays* in the beautiful Big Sky Country of Montana. Guests included Art Garfunkel, Ed Begley Jr., and Dennis Weaver.

April 1987—I shot an American Express ad with Annie Leibovitz, the renowned, iconic photographer. The shoot took place at a pond just after dawn on a chilly Tennessee spring morning. Annie wanted to capture me "dancing on water," so a Lucite table was placed just beneath the pond's surface. She told me to close my eyes and dance. My sense of balance wasn't great to begin with, and I was four months pregnant. While I didn't fall over completely, I struggled to look graceful and poised with my feet in freezing cold water. The experience was magical, watching an artist manipulating her medium, which just happened to be me.

Spring to Summer 1987—Focused on songwriting during my pregnancy with Matt. During a stay in the hospital for preterm labor (July–August), I received a song from Jimmy Webb called "If These Walls Could Speak." I also conducted my one and only interview to find a suitable nanny.

September 1, 1987—Phyllis Mayfield moved from Amarillo, Texas, to Riverstone Farm. She has been a constant presence in my children's lives.

September 1987—Tracking for my next album, *Lead Me On*, began as I entered my ninth month of pregnancy. I'll never forget the glorious chaos of the time right around Matt's birth. I love to cook and had agreed to cater a party at my sister Mimi's house. Later that night I went to record the music for the song "Lead Me On." It was then that Gary told me that our doctor had called and wanted to induce me the next morning—we had an 8 a.m.

appointment to deliver our first child. On September 25, I gave birth to Matthew Garrison Chapman. Later that afternoon, Brown called from the studio to check the right key for the song "Shadows." A few days later I was back in the studio. It sounds crazy, but everything came together in a very fluid, organic way. Music, family, and life events flowed into and out of each other naturally.

Spring 1988—*Lead Me On,* my eleventh project, launched. From June 1988 through August 1989, the *Lead Me On* tour, a joint billing with Michael W. Smith and myself, covered over 150 cities. Along with band and crew buses, a family bus was added for the first time. In fact, Matt learned to walk on our bus. Included in the band: Gary Chapman, Michael W. Smith, Chris Eaton, Chris Rodriguez, Jerry McPherson, Ken Rarick, Warren Ham, Terry McMillan, Greg Morrow, and Donna McElroy.

June 1989—I met Jennifer Cooke backstage at the Pacific Amphitheatre in California. Within a few months she joined the management team.

December 16, 1989—I gave birth to Gloria Mills Chapman.

1990—I concentrated on spending time with Matt and Millie, songwriting, and recording. My upcoming project involved three producers: Brown Bannister and Keith Thomas in Nashville and Michael Omartian in L.A. (up until this point, I had worked with Brown exclusively). In the fall, Gary and I hosted the first of a series of youth gatherings called "The Loft" at our farm in Franklin, Tennessee. Our volunteer counselors, the "grayshirts," interacted with over five hundred kids every week. We would host this event for several more years to come and eventually recorded *Songs from the Loft.*

1991—*Heart in Motion,* project number twelve, was released in the spring. The next fifteen months included the making of five videos, an international tour, a one-hundred-city U.S. tour (our band included Chris Eaton, Chris Rodriguez, Jerry McPherson, Mari Falcone, Terome "T-Bone" Hannon, Chris McHugh, Renee Garcia, and Nicole Coleman [Mullin]), and a tour staff of over one hundred people, including nannies, children, and extended family.

February 1992—I gave my second performance on the Grammys, singing "Baby Baby." Two-year-old Millie, my inspiration for the song, joined me on stage.

June and July 1992—Recorded my second Christmas album, *Home for Christmas*.

October 11, 1992—I gave birth to Sarah Cannon Chapman. Shortly after *Home for Christmas* released, baby Sarah accompanied me on all the holiday promotions. I remember being on *The Tonight Show with Jay Leno*. Jay worked so hard to get Sarah to smile but to no avail. She saved her first smile for me on Christmas Eve morning.

1993—The first half of 1993 was spent at home with Matt, Millie, and Sarah as I started the songwriting process for the next record, *House of Love*, with producers Michael Omartian and Keith Thomas. A&M decided to create a documentary of the making of this record so producer Jim Shea and a film crew followed me around for almost a year. The result was called *Building the House of Love*.

December 1993—Three separate projects that involved working with Vince Gill all coincided in this month: a Christmas television special he hosted from Tulsa that included me as a guest (along with Michael MacDonald and Chet Atkins); the first of a series of benefit concerts, conducted by Ronn Huff, that I hosted to raise money for the Nashville Symphony featuring Vince, Michael W. Smith, and Gary Chapman as guests; and Vince's acceptance of my invitation to sing high harmony on the title track of the new record, "House of Love." We hit it off so well and worked so easily together that I jokingly told him that if I'd been born a boy, we'd have been best friends.

Early 1994—*House of Love* released.

May 1, 1994—I received the Pax Christi award at St. John's University. The program was recorded for a PBS Mother's Day special and a live CD.

Summer 1994 to Fall 1995—Wayne Kirkpatrick was hired as tour producer for the *House of Love* tour. The band included Wayne, Jerry McPherson, Will Owsley, Rick Palombi, Millard Powers, Chris McHugh, Kim Keyes, and Tabitha Fair. We spent six weeks in production rehearsals, longer than any tour I'd done. Touring began in Southeast Asia and included over one hundred cities worldwide.

Summer 1995—I made a sentimental return trip to Caribou Ranch for two days of songwriting. "Takes a Little Time" was one of the songs inspired there. Between tour dates, I invested concentrated time on songwriting with one of my favorite co-writers, Wayne Kirkpatrick. Our favorite writing spot: the rustic hilltop cabins at Hidden Trace Farm in Franklin, Tennessee, which I had purchased in spring of 1994.

1996 to 1997—*Behind the Eyes,* a new recording project, was underway. Over thirty songs were written and recorded by two producers, Wayne Kirkpatrick and Keith Thomas.

Spring 1997—I shot a "Milk Mustache" ad with Annie Leibovitz outside of Bakersfield, California. During a break, Annie photographed my seven-year-old daughter Millie and me. Later Annie sent me several haunting mother-daughter photos as a gift.

Fall 1997—*Behind the Eyes,* my fifteenth project, released. I spent most of October doing overseas promotion before returning home for a holiday Christmas tour with the Nashville Symphony. My guests were Michael W. Smith and CeCe Winans.

Spring and Summer 1998—I toured over sixty cities promoting *Behind the Eyes.* Our band included Tommy Sims, Mark Harris, Dan Needham, Andrew Ramsey, Jerry McPherson, Kim Keyes, Tabitha Fair, and Tim Lauer. After Thanksgiving I enjoyed a second Christmas tour with the Nashville Symphony.

February 1999—Gary and I separated with the intention of divorce.

June 1999—Divorce final. I filmed the CBS made-for-TV movie, *Song from the Heart,* in Vancouver, British Columbia. My first serious acting role came at a time when I was grateful to inhabit someone else's life rather than my own.

Summer 1999—I recorded my third Christmas album, *A Christmas to Remember,* with Pat Williams and Michael Omartian. It released as my sixteenth recording project in the fall. I also filmed my second television Christmas special in Banff, Canada, with guests Tony Bennett, CeCe Winans, and 98 Degrees.

Friday afternoon, March 10, 2000—Vince and I were married standing on the hillside by the cabins. I was barefoot.

Summer 2000 to Spring 2001—I began working on several new projects, writing songs and tracking for the next record, and preparing for baby Gill. Keith Thomas had agreed to produce the new album, *Simple Things,* but singing was a little more difficult being pregnant at forty. The project was put on hold.

March 12, 2001—I gave birth to Corrina Grant Gill, the youngest of our blended family of five.

January 2002—I decided to set aside production of *Simple Things* and record a collection of hymns. Produced by Brown Bannister and Vince, this project galvanized the rich heritage of hymns with this new season of my life. It was a special time with Vince as we were immersed in so much of the music that shaped my life. Past and present converged in this important time of reconnection for me to my musical roots and to my faith.

Spring 2002—*Legacy...Hymns and Faith* released. Our tour schedule was lighter than in years past. Included in the band: Vince Gill, Tim Akers, Mark Oakley, Gary Lunn, John Hammond, Kim Keyes, and Melody Crittenden.

December 2002—Christmas tour with Vince and Nashville Chamber Orchestra, conducted by David Hamilton.

January 2003—Released *Simple Things,* my eighteenth project, and toured with Mercy Me and Bebo Norman. Our band included Will Owsley, Mark Oakley, Jonathan Hamby, Millard Powers, Chris McHugh, and Kim Keyes.

December 2003—Christmas tour with Vince and Nashville Chamber Orchestra, conducted by David Hamilton.

Fall 2004—Released *Greatest Hits.*

December 2004—Christmas tour with Vince and Nashville Chamber Orchestra, conducted by David Hamilton.

2005—*Rock of Ages,* a second collection of hymns, released as project number twenty.

February 2005—I was asked by NBC to host a philanthropic reality show produced by Andrew Glassman and Jason Raff. If I could have sculpted a program that involved celebrating community, fulfilling the dreams of people in need, and doing music (I gave free concerts in all the towns we visited), I couldn't have done better than *Three Wishes*. From April to December, I filmed thirteen episodes. While it was some of the most exhausting physical work I've ever done, it was emotionally fulfilling.

Fall 2005—*Three Wishes* aired on NBC for one season.

April 2006—I recorded a retrospective live concert at Bass Hall in Fort Worth, Texas, a conscious nod to my first live ticketed event some twenty-five-plus years earlier. My band included Jonathan Hamby, Kim Keyes, Gene Miller, Will Owsley, Millard Powers, and Jim Bogios…and most recently, Tony Harrell, Doli Stepnewski, and Dan Needham.

2007—I spent most of the year at the cabins writing songs (yet to be recorded) and pieces for this book.

They say hindsight is twenty-twenty. On paper the direction of my life seems so clear. The experience of it, however, has felt much more like a twisting, curving road full of surprises. My passion has always been the connecting power of music, connecting us to each other, to ourselves, and to the love of God.

I wonder where the next chapter will lead…

DISCOGRAPHY

ALBUMS AND VIDEOS

Since 1978, Amy Grant has sold more than twenty-five million albums worldwide, including one Quintuple Platinum, one Triple Platinum, one Double Platinum, as well as six Platinum (one million sold) and four Gold (five hundred thousand sold).

Amy Grant	1978	album	
My Father's Eyes	1979	album	Gold
Never Alone	1980	album	
In Concert	1981	album	
In Concert Volume Two	1981	album	
Age to Age	1982	album	Platinum
A Christmas Album	1983	album	Platinum
The Age to Age Concert	1983	full-length video	
Straight Ahead	1984	album	Platinum
Unguarded	1985	album	Platinum
"Angels"	1985	music video	
"It's Not a Song"	1985	music video	
The Collection	1986	album	Platinum
Find a Way	1986	full-length video	Gold
"Find a Way"	1986	music video	
"Wise Up"	1986	music video	
Lead Me On	1988	album	Platinum
"Next Time I Fall"	1988	music video	
"Stay for Awhile"	1988	music video	
"Lead Me On"	1989	music video	

Heart in Motion .... 1991 ..... album .... Quintuple Platinum

"Baby Baby" .... 1991 ..... music video

"Every Heartbeat" .... 1991 ..... music video

"That's What
     Love Is For" .... 1991 ..... music video

Home for Christmas .... 1992 ..... album .... Triple Platinum

Heart in Motion
     Video Collection .... 1992 ..... full-length video .... Gold

Old Fashioned Christmas ..... 1992 ..... full-length video .... Gold

"Good for Me" .... 1992 ..... music video

"I Will Remember You" ..... 1992 ..... music video

"Grown Up
     Christmas List" .... 1992 ..... music video

House of Love .... 1994 ..... album .... Double Platinum

Building the House of Love .... 1994 ..... full-length video

"Lucky One" .... 1994 ..... music video

"House of Love" .... 1994 ..... music video

"Say You'll Be Mine" .... 1994 ..... music video

"Things We Do
     for Love" .... 1996 ..... music video

Behind the Eyes .... 1997 ..... album .... Gold

"Takes a Little Time" .... 1997 ..... music video

A Christmas to Remember .... 1999 ..... album .... Gold

Legacy...Hymns & Faith ...... 2002 ..... album .... Gold

Legacy...Hymns & Faith ...... 2002 ..... full-length video

Greatest Inspirational Songs ... 2002 ..... album

Simple Things .... 2003 ..... album

"Simple Things" .... 2003 ..... music video

Greatest Hits 1986–2004 ..... 2004 ..... album

Rock of Ages...
     Hymns & Faith .... 2005 ..... album

Time Again...
    Amy Grant Live .... 2006 ..... album
Time Again...
    Amy Grant Live .... 2006 ..... full-length video
Amy Grant's Greatest Hits .... 2007 ..... album

Awards and Achievements

Grammy Awards and Nominations

1982 .... award .... Best Gospel Performance, ... "Age to Age"
Contemporary

1983 .... award .... Best Gospel Performance, Female .... "Ageless Medley"

1984 .... award .... Best Gospel Performance, Female .... "Angels"

1985 .... award .... Best Gospel Performance, Female .... "Unguarded"

1988 .... award .... Best Gospel Performance, Female .... "Lead Me On"

1992 .... nomination .... Best Pop Performance, Female .... "Baby Baby"

1992 .... nomination .... Record of the Year .... "Baby Baby"

1992 .... nomination .... Song of the Year .... "Baby Baby"

1992 .... nomination .... Album of the Year .... *Heart in Motion*

1994 .... nomination .... Children's Spoken Word .... *Lion and the Lamb*, with Christopher Reeve

2005 .... award .... Best Southern, Country or .... *Rock of Ages...*
Bluegrass Gospel Album *Hymns & Faith*

Dove Awards

1983 .... Artist of the Year .... Amy Grant

1983 .... Pop/Contemporary Album of the Year .... *Age to Age*

1983 .... Recorded Music Packaging of the Year .... *Age to Age*

1984 .... Recorded Music Packaging of the Year .... *A Christmas Album*

1985 .... Pop/Contemporary Album of the Year .... *Straight Ahead*

1986 .... Artist of the Year .... Amy Grant

1986 .... Recorded Music Packaging of the Year .... *Unguarded*

1988 .... Short Form Video of the Year .... "Stay for Awhile"

1989 .... Artist of the Year .... Amy Grant

1989 .... Pop/Contemporary Album of the Year .... *Lead Me On*

1989 .... Short Form Video Music Video of the Year ... "Lead Me On"

1990 .... Country Recorded Song of the Year .... *Tis So Sweet to Trust in Jesus*

1992 .... Song of the Year .... "Place in This World"

1992 .... Artist of the Year .... Amy Grant

1994 .... Praise and Worship Album of the Year .... *Songs from the Loft*

1996 .... Special Event Album of the Year .... *My Utmost for His Highest*

1998 .... Pop/Contemporary Album of the Year .... *Behind the Eyes*

2000 .... Special Event Album of the Year .... *Streams*

2003 .... Inspirational Album of the Year .... *Legacy...Hymns & Faith*

2003 .... Country Recorded Song of the Year .... "The River's Gonna Keep on Rolling"

2006 .... Inspirational Album of the Year .... *Rock of Ages... Hymns & Faith*

2007 .... Long Form Music Video of the Year .... *Time Again... Amy Grant Live*

SOME OF AMY'S SPECIAL AWARDS AND ACHIEVEMENTS

1992 .... Young Tennessean of the Year .... Junior Chamber of Commerce

1994 .... Pax Christi Award .... St. John University

1994 .... Harmony Award .... Nashville Symphony

1996 .... Golden Plate Award .... Academy of Achievement

1996 .... Minnie Pearl Humanitarian Award .... Columbia Hospital

1996 .... Sarah Cannon Humanitarian Award .... TNN

1996 .... Voice of America Award .... ASCAP

1999 .... "An Evening with the Arts," honoring .... Nashville Performing Arts
         Amy Grant's contribution to
         the Nashville Performing Arts

1999 .... Amy Grant rose is named

1999 .... Amy Grant Room for Music and Entertainment is dedicated
         at the Target House, a family-support facility at St. Jude
         Children's Hospital in Memphis, Tennessee

2001 .... Nashvillian of the Year .... Easter Seals

2002 .... Star on the Hollywood Walk of Fame .... Hollywood Chamber
                                                       of Commerce (actual
                                                       dedication ceremony
                                                       in 2006)

2003 .... Inducted into the Gospel Music Hall of Fame

2003 .... 25th Anniversary Award for Membership .... ASCAP

2003 .... Summit Award .... Estes Park Seminar
                                                       in the Rockies

2006 .... Amy Grant Performance Platform named .... Nashville, TN
         at the grand opening of the Schermerhorn
         Symphony Center

2007 .... Charter member of Tiffany Circle .... Red Cross

Rights and Permissions

"1974 (We Were Young)" by Amy Grant, Jerry McPherson, and Gary Chapman © 1988 Age to Age Music Inc. (ASCAP) / Riverstone Music (ASCAP) (both admin. by The Loving Company), Word Music LLC (ASCAP). All rights reserved. Used by permission.

"After the Fire" by Amy Grant © 1998 Age to Age Music Inc. (ASCAP) / Riverstone Music (ASCAP) (both admin. by The Loving Company). All rights reserved. Used by permission.

"All Right" by Amy Grant, Dann Huff, and Phil Naish © 1988 Word Music LLC / Dayspring Music LLC (ASCAP), Ashlyne Music (BMI) (admin. by Word Music LLC), Pamela Kay Music / Beckengus Music (ASCAP) (both admin. by EMI Christian Music Group Inc.). BMG Music. All rights reserved. Used by permission.

"Angels" by Amy Grant, Gary Chapman, Michael W. Smith, and Brown Bannister © 1984 Word Music LLC (ASCAP), Meadowgreen Music Company (ASCAP) (admin. by EMI Christian Music Group Inc.), BMG Songs Inc. All rights reserved. Used by permission.

"Ask Me" by Amy Grant and Tom Hemby © 1991 Age to Age Music Inc. (ASCAP) / Riverstone Music (ASCAP) (both admin. by The Loving Company), BMG Songs Inc. (ASCAP) / Puxico Music (ASCAP) (admin. by BMG Songs Inc.). All rights reserved. Used by permission.

"Baby Baby" by Amy Grant and Keith Thomas © 1991 Age to Age Music Inc. (ASCAP) / Riverstone Music (ASCAP) (both admin. by The Loving Company), Dimensional Music of 1091 (ASCAP) (admin. by Cherry Lane Music Pub. Co., BMG Songs Inc. (BMI). All rights reserved. Used by permission.

Tunes LLC (ASCAP) (admin. by Sony / ATV Music Publishing,
8 Music Square West, Nashville, TN 37203). All rights reserved.
Used by permission.

"Mimi's House" by Amy Grant © 1981 Word Music LLC (ASCAP).
All rights reserved. Used by permission.

"Missing You" by Amy Grant © 1997 Age to Age Music Inc. (ASCAP) /
Riverstone Music (ASCAP) (both admin. by The Loving Company).
All rights reserved. Used by permission.

"Oh Tennessee" by Amy Grant © 2007 Grant Girls Music LLC (admin.
by The Loving Company). All rights reserved. Used by permission.

"Out in the Open" by Amy Grant and Chris Eaton © 2003 Grant Girls
Music LLC (ASCAP) (admin. by The Loving Company), Dayspring
Music LLC (BMI) / SGO Music Publishing Ltd. (BMI) (admin. by
Dayspring Music LLC). All rights reserved. Used by permission.

"Saved by Love" by Amy Grant, Justin Peters, and Chris Smith © 1988
Word Music LLC (ASCAP), Justin Peters Music (BMI) (admin.
by Songs for the Planet Inc., P.O. Box 40251, Nashville, TN 37204),
Dennis Morgan Music (a div. of Morgan Music Group) (BMI).
All rights reserved. Used by permission.

"Say Once More" by Amy Grant and Gardner Cole © 1980 Word Music
LLC (ASCAP), Warner-Tamerlane Publishing Corp. (BMI) / Sizzling
Blue Music (BMI) (admin. by Warner-Tamerlane Publishing Corp.).
All rights reserved. Used by permission.

"Somewhere Down the Road" by Amy Grant and Wayne Kirkpatrick
© 1997 Age to Age Music Inc. (ASCAP) / Riverstone Music (ASCAP)
(both admin. by The Loving Company), Warner-Tamerlane Publishing
Corp. (BMI), Sell the Cow Music (BMI) (admin. by Warner-Tamerlane
Publishing Corp.). All rights reserved. Used by permission.

"Takes a Little Time" by Amy Grant and Wayne Kirkpatrick © 1997 Age
to Age Music Inc. (ASCAP) / Riverstone Music (ASCAP) (both
admin. by The Loving Company), Careers–BMG Music Pub. Inc.

© Deborah Feingold

Amy Grant is the bestselling Christian music artist of all time and the first to cross over and garner the number one spot on Billboard's pop charts. Since beginning her career at age fifteen she has earned six Grammy Awards, twenty-six Dove Awards, and has sold more than thirty million records worldwide. In 2006 she received a star on the Hollywood Walk of Fame. Amy lives in Nashville, Tennessee with her husband, country music star Vince Gill, and their five children.